He's Not Interested, He's Just Passing Time

40 Unmistakable Behaviors of Men Who Avoid Commitment and Play Games with Women

By Bruce Bryans

www.BruceBryans.com

Legal Disclaimer

ISBN-13: 978-1518892103

ISBN-10: 1518892108

Table of Contents

Introduction

Truth time: Men don't really have "commitment issues." At least, not in the way most women think men do. When a man tells you that he has "commitment issues", he either means one of two things:

1. He's placed a high price on his loyalty and is therefore very reluctant to offer you his commitment because he's not yet convinced of your value to him, or…

2. He's not that interested and is just passing time with you.

If it's the first reason, you have some influence over the situation because as you interact with him, only time will tell if your Mr. McDreamy will eventually see you as the kind of woman he can give his all to. This is normal. Especially for higher quality men who recognize their high value, as they'll require a good amount of time to determine if you're "The One."

However, if it's the second reason, you have zero influence on the situation. Why? Because if a guy is not that interested in you, his "commitment issues" are nothing more than an excuse to waste your time and reap the benefits of your decision to stay with him in order to "see where this thing goes."

In general, even though men are more than able to commit to a woman once certain conditions in their life are met (most of which will have nothing to do with you, by the way), they will not directly *tell you* that no matter what you do or say, you're not going to get the commitment you want. Few guys will rarely ever come out and *inform you* when you're not the right girl for them or that now isn't the right time for them to take a woman seriously. I mean, why should they? We live in a culture where, **predominantly**, dating with marriage as the primary goal is more of an afterthought. Instead, today's culture glorifies romantic love (the most fleeting of them all) as the end all be all, and that anything is better than being single and alone, including hooking up with random strangers.

So if this is the culture men live in (the very same culture that tends to evaluate manhood based on how successful a man is at seducing women), what's to stop a guy from dating you casually, playing with your emotions, and wasting your time when he's fully aware that you're nothing more than a beautiful distraction or a brag-worthy conquest?

Honestly, I don't enjoy painting such a grim picture of the dating landscape because it's really not all that bad. Not every guy out there is going to consciously go out of his way to waste his time with a woman knowing full well that he's only with her to pass the time. You do have some great guys out there that actually *want* to meet the right woman and someday build a life with her. However, even the "good" guys might be unaware that their dating decisions aren't solely based on their good intentions. It's also based on the influences of modern culture.

A great guy, one with seemingly nobler aims, might still engage in casual flings or non-committal relationships with unsuspecting women. Why? Well, for many reasons. Sometimes it's because he knows his peers are judging him and that their respect for him is tied directly to how well he does with the opposite sex. Sometimes it's because he's so focused on his career ambitions that he needs a beautiful distraction to help him unwind from time to time, even if he knows this beautiful distraction is a short-term one. And sometimes it's just because he actually doesn't know what he wants, but he'd rather keep you around until he figures it out (which he usually does much later and at your expense; when he realizes that he's just not that interested in you).

No matter which way you look at it, even though men don't really have commitment issues, they don't find it necessary or in *their* best interest to inform a woman when she's nothing more than a beautiful distraction, a way to earn the respect of his peers, or just a target to sharpen his seduction skills so that he'll be primed and ready when a "better" woman comes along.

This is the ugly truth, but there's hope.

This sort of male behavior is actually *easy* to spot IF you know what to look for. It's extremely difficult for a man to waste your time and treat you like a short-term fling without exhibiting certain unmistakable behaviors that clearly communicate that he's trying to keep you interested…but unclaimed.

A Small Caveat: Be Reasonable

Keep in mind that the list of behaviors in this book is mainly focused on guys who are hesitant or unwilling to make you their girlfriend. If you're searching for a list of reasons why a man won't commit specifically to marriage, I've written a little book called, *101 Reasons*

Why He Won't Commit To You, that details many of those same reasons. Committing to marriage brings up a different set of fears and insecurities in men altogether. So to keep things in perspective, keep in mind that this list will focus on men who have issues making the jump from casual dating to becoming (and staying) exclusive with you.

Also keep in mind that human beings (men included) are a lot more complex than we'd like to admit. Add to that the fact that we live in a world where our needs and desires are sure to conflict with the needs and desires of others. Men, just like women, aren't perfect and are therefore subject to errors in judgment. So with that in mind, I want you to consider that **just because a man isn't quick to offer you a commitment, it doesn't mean that he's _intentionally_ trying to use you.** It could simply mean that he's just not convinced that you're "The One" yet or that there's some other reason that might be compelling him to take things very slow with you.

It's important to look at your situation carefully and use your own judgment and female intuition (something I discuss later in the book) when it comes to determining whether or not a man is being genuine with you or being manipulative. Use the guidelines in this book to help you assess and confirm your own suspicions or concerns. I'll be the first to admit that romantic relationships can be insanely complicated to navigate, and determining someone's intentions is rarely ever as easy as going through a list of behaviors. So again, I say this with nothing but love and sincerity: Use the checklist as a set of guidelines, but be willing to look at your situation with a man objectively.

For example, a man might withdraw from you all of a sudden because of a major change in his career. If he's been expecting a big promotion (the kind that would make him a more confident provider) but doesn't get it, it may cause him to redouble his efforts on his career...at your expense. In a situation like this, you're going to have to use the guidelines in this book in conjunction with your own judgment to decide if his low interest means, *"I'm not that interested in you"* or *"I need you to be patient with me during this time."*

The Three Types of Men

Obviously, depending on the discussion at hand there is always going to be more than three types of men. However, for the purpose of determining if a man is unfit or unwilling to commit, we're going to place men in three categories: Men who want and see a future with you, men who don't want or see a future with you, and men who aren't sure of what they want yet or who's life plans/time schedules don't align with your own.

This book is meant to help you decipher between the first and second group so that you can end up with a man from the first group sooner than later on in life. This is the easy part. However, things get a little bit trickier when it comes to the third group.

In the previous section, I stressed the point of using your own judgment and female intuition because there will be situations where a man is not "intentional" about wasting your time. Health issues, financial issues, social pressures, the loss of a loved one or even the loss of a job, etc. could quickly cause a man to shift his focus *away* from a romantic relationship, especially one in its infancy. In circumstances like this he might not want to lose you, but he might also realize that he needs a bit more space to get his stuff together.

Of course, none of these things are *your* problem, and you don't have any obligation to stick it out with a guy who's going through a rough time, especially if you've been dating less than two months. Keep in mind though that it might not be the noblest decision a woman can make if she decides to bail on a guy the minute life deals him a rough hand. But then again, if his "rough time" is a product of his own vices it could be a huge red flag telling you that you need to get out as quickly as you can. You need to approach these dating situations with a lot of discretion and practical wisdom in order to make the right decision.

The Women That Need This Book

If you find that you have little to no problem attracting men, but seem to have a ton of issues making them take you seriously (because you entertain Time Wasters), this book is for you. If you also seem to have trouble deciphering the intentions of the men you date (much to your chagrin later on), this book is for you. Even if men do take you seriously and you do understand men, yet you somehow always end up in dead-end relationships with half-committed or emotionally unavailable men…this book is for you.

Now, even though we've defined the problem, we still need to properly define the kind of woman I truly want to help with this book. I write all of my books with a particular woman in mind; those with sincere hearts, lots of love and respect to give, and who have a deep desire to find a high-quality, commitment-ready man to build a life with. I do this to ensure that the advice I give pertaining to how men think is not abused or misused by women.

So with all that said, here are two ways to know if this book will benefit you or not:

1. You want to attract and keep the attention of a high-quality man (a man with high self-esteem, ambition, leadership qualities, compassion, cherishes commitment, has high-standards for himself, defends his personal boundaries, knows what he wants, speaks his mind, understands the value of relationships, and exudes masculine, sexual confidence).

2. You want to pursue and nurture a *loving relationship that can lead to marriage* with such a man.

If you're not interested in dating guys that will hold you to a high but reasonable standard (meaning he won't tolerate flaky or disrespectful behavior) or if you're not interested in securing a serious relationship with a masculine man who wants and values commitment…this book is not for you. If you want to attract one-night stands, so called "players", or forty something year-old bad boys who think commitment is just another curse word…this book is not for you.

Commit-minded, high-quality men date consciously and sagaciously so as to weed through the innumerous amount of low-character, low-chemistry, or incompatible women in order to find their Miss Right. They are **less likely** to waste a woman's time because their time is extremely precious to them. Because they value commitment, relationships, social ties, and family very highly, they date with the intention of finding a woman they can build a life with, one who is willing to support their life's mission.

So if you want to learn how to decipher between men who only want you for a moment versus the man who wants you for a lifetime, I encourage you to read on.

Chapter One:

He'll Never Make You His Girlfriend

1

He's emotionally unavailable.

The emotionally unavailable man is the man who is simply not emotionally invested in you enough to keep you around for the long haul of a serious relationship. A subclass of the emotionally unavailable man is the one who likes you just enough to get his needs met, but not enough to ensure that you get yours met. If you have that nauseating or nagging gut-feeling (woman's intuition) that you can fall off the face of the earth without him realizing it until a few days later...he's clearly not interested in whatever it is you two have at the moment (I wouldn't insult you by calling it a relationship).

The main thing about dating an emotionally unavailable man is that he'll never provide you with the kind of emotional intimacy that gives you the security you crave. Women crave the security that men provide, in all of its varied forms, and the emotionally unavailable man is the one who will most assuredly rob you of the kind of emotional fulfillment that only a man who is willing to be "all in" and vulnerable with you can offer.

The biggest problem with being with an emotionally unavailable man is that his words and actions tends to confuse women, leading them to believe that there could possibly be a future with him. Because of this, many women fail to recognize the flashing signs that men like this give off, especially earlier on in a new romance.

Let me explain why.

First of all, when a man shuts himself off from love it doesn't mean that he's emotionally dead. This confuses women a lot because they assume that an affectionate, caring man – one who will call her when she's sick, and enjoys meeting her friends and going out together, etc. – cannot possibly be emotionally unavailable.

False.

Instead of equating emotionally unavailability with emotional deadness, equate it with not being "all in", vulnerable, willing to fall in love, or showing a desire to claim you as his very own. A guy can have a heart of gold, show you a good time, and give you more butterflies in your stomach than your first high school crush, but if he doesn't want to claim you or end up as **your boyfriend** you're headed towards a dead-end.

Emotionally unavailable men will *seem* as if they're sending conflicting messages when they're really not. What they've done is simply *informed* you that they "don't want anything serious" or that "they're just looking for something casual" and you've mistaken their affection and attentiveness as being their true feelings for you.

Wrong.

If a man clearly tells you that he doesn't want anything serious and you give him the green light by seeing him anyway, his affection and attentiveness isn't a contradiction to his declaration of unattainability, it's merely him *enjoying* you (and the benefits that come with you) for the moment. If he tells you upfront that he won't give you want you want – a commitment – believe him. His apparent interest in you is not an indication that he has or is in the process of changing his mind.

In cases like this it's always best to take a man at his word. If he uses sketchy language that clearly or subtly illustrates a half-hearted interest in you, don't rationalize the situation by telling yourself that you'll "see where this thing goes." Why? Well, because it won't go anywhere at all, which shouldn't be a surprise to you since he's already indicated this outcome.

When a man's declarations of unattainability contradict his behavior, it has the potential to escalate a woman's desire for him. This then compels her to work twice as hard to secure his unattainable commitment, much to her chagrin. If you don't take anything else from this book, keep this in mind: Falling for the ambiguous interest of a **highly desirable man** will make you addicted to chasing him, and you'll find yourself doing whatever you possibly can to change his mind.

2

He hides information from you.

If a man is going out of his way to hide information from you, this should be a huge red flag that he's probably not interested in anything long-term with you. Admittedly however, this one is a bit difficult to navigate. Just because he doesn't allow you to peruse through his phone when you want, or just because he doesn't reveal everything about himself and his life right away doesn't mean that he's not taking you seriously. The only way to really tell if his quest to conceal information from you is a red flag or not is to look at it in the context of the relationship stage you are in with him.

If you're just getting to know a guy and he's adamant about keeping certain aspects of his life private from you for the time being, this is normal. He could be embarrassed about whatever subject it is you're asking him about or he may simply be uncomfortable revealing certain things about his life to a woman that he hasn't fully emotionally invested in yet.

Even when it comes to their cell phones, most guys aren't going to simply grant you full access to this magical little woman management device at the outset of a new romance (yes, that is what it is to many single men). In all honesty, he may still be "testing the waters" other women and might actually be in the process ₀eciding which girl deserves his full and undivided attention.

The problem starts however, when things begin to get a bit more serious. If you've been dating for several weeks or months and you've already expressed your desire for exclusivity, there's usually no reason for him to act sketchy and avoidant when it comes to important details about his life. At this particular stage, he shouldn't even be afraid to let you use his cell phone if you really need to make a call, etc. Of course, if you've been exhibiting overly distrusting, privacy invading girlfriend behavior, a man may opt to keep you as far away from certain aspects of his life just to avoid an incident.

3

You're always the one to initiate contact.

Have you ever found yourself as the "Initiator" in a relationship, where you were always the one to call, text, or email? Do you remember how foolish you felt the day you realized that your enthusiasm to get in touch with someone you wanted to be with was not mutual? I remember. We've all been there (most of us at least), and it's a terrible feeling when you realize that if you got kidnapped, the other person probably wouldn't know until your picture showed up on the news.

Consider it a clear red flag that you're just an "option" or a girl to pass the time with if you're always the one to initiate contact with a man. Why? Because when a man, a mature man, is enthusiastic about a woman he makes his presence clear and consistent through his willingness to get in touch, and keep in touch, with her.

As I say in my book, _Never Chase Men Again_, as a relationship between you and Mr. McDreamy begins to develop, it will be to your best advantage _not_ to always be the one who initiates contact between the two of you. If you find yourself in a position where you are **predominantly** the first one to text, call, and make plans, you're playing the ugly game of Chase-a-Man. Letting a man dominate the initiation of contact is the only sure way you can gauge his level of interest in you.

He isn't eager or proactive about seeing you again.

When a man is "on the fence" about you, only half-interested in you, or simply looking to pass the time with you, his efforts to make plans to see you again after a date will be almost assuredly _passive_. Of course, if a guy does this after the first date he may simply be trying to play "hard-to-get" and doesn't want to look too eager and therefore, desperate. However, if you've already gone out with this guy two or more times and he still takes forever and a day to connect with you…he's probably not that interested.

But why would he still contact you and make plans (usually a week or more later) if he's not *that* interested? Well, he could be bored and probably doesn't mind a beautiful distraction like you in his life just for the moment. If he's the player type, he might even be juggling several women at the same time and has decided to keep you on the backburner until a "better" spot opens up. Clearly, neither of these are situations that you'll want to find yourself in, since it's stupidly obvious that the only attention a guy like this will give you will be half-hearted and insincere at best.

This might be common sense, but let me say it anyway: After actually going out on two or more dates with you, when a guy is *really* attracted to you and feels an undeniable amount of chemistry, he will make his intentions to spend more time with you ridiculously clear. You won't have to guess, stress, and refresh your inbox every eight seconds…you'll know.

5

He doesn't introduce you to his friends and family.

This one is a major, super major red flag. It's so major that it should be common sense to all women by now. Unless he's just moved to a new city, there is virtually no excuse you can give for the guy you're seeing if he's never introduced you to his friends or family and you've been dating for quite some time.

Now, to explain how men think and behave in this regard I'm going to have to drop some ugly truth bombs. So gird your loins.

Here's the thing. It may seem shallow to the uninitiated woman, but men gain deep satisfaction from being able to attract the attention, respect, and adoration of women. But even more so, men gain fulfillment in being able to prove to others (their social circles) that they're capable of attracting a high-value and highly attractive woman. Regardless of what a man may think of himself, the quality of his manhood is, and has been since our hunter-gatherer days, a product of what the *other* men think of him, particularly the men he spends the majority of his time with. This means that a guy is only going to introduce you to his friends and family if he believes doing so won't lead to social humiliation, scorn, or **dishonor** among *the men*.

Confused? Let me simplify…

He won't introduce you to his friends and family if he's just passing time with you. And if he's just passing time with you, you're obviously not his "ideal" woman – the woman he's proud and honored to be with. This, my dear, is the ugly, ugly truth about men and how they decide which woman is worth bringing home to friends and family.

I mention all this to illustrate how men play the dating game and how their family and friends factor into this aspect of their lives. The reality is, the more long-term value you have to a man the more enthusiastic he'll be towards showing you off to his friends and family.

Of course, if he's hyper vigilant about keeping you away from his family it could mean that he has some family issues that he's ashamed of and wants to keep you as far away from them as humanly possible. This is understandable to a degree. So if you think this might be the case you should gracefully ask him about it. Fortunately, if he feels particularly comfortable opening up to you he might admit to being embarrassed of his family. But keep in mind that even though we cannot choose our family, we can still choose our friends. So if you've been dating a man for a while and he hasn't introduced you to his friends at least…it's quite possible that he's not interested in a future with you.

Don't rationalize the situation or second-guess yourself on this. If you honestly get a gut feeling that the guy you're seeing is ashamed of you, you can bet he's playing hard-core defense to keep you away from his friends and family. But why would he go through such lengths instead of being upfront with you? Well, it's because he either wants something from you or he doesn't want to lose what he's already getting. He also knows that the more he integrates you into his world the harder it's going to be for him to get rid of you after he's lost interest in whatever it is you had to offer him.

6

He doesn't show any interest in meeting your friends and family.

So you've been seeing a whole lot of a guy and you're pretty sure he's profoundly smitten with you. You can't stop thinking about him and you love spending time with him. In fact, time seems to fly when you're together and sparks fly in every direction when you're in close quarters. So why then, after two to three months of non-stop dating, he seems to be vehemently against the idea of meeting your friends and family?

Short answer: If it seems to good to be true it probably is. Your Mr. McDreamy might be nothing more than a passing romantic fancy, enjoying his time with you to be sure, but definitely not interested in pursuing you for anything long-term.

To avoid completely disappointing you or scaring you off with his disinterest in meeting your friends and family, he may use a reasonable excuse like his hectic work schedule. He might even try a more dramatic approach and make it seem as if you're being unreasonable, as he argues that you're moving too fast by having him meet your loved ones "so soon." If he's a real master manipulator he might even tell you he just wants to enjoy the alluring mystery of your romance a little while longer, mentioning that bringing family or friends into the picture might ruin the magic. As you can see, some men are certified masterminds and have an endless bag of seductive tricks when it comes to getting their way with women.

Naturally, you need to be able to weed through your guy's brand of manipulative rubbish to see the situation for what it really is: He's just not that interested in anything long-term with you. Any guy who finds you a spectacular catch won't be averse to meeting your friends and family, assuming you're not trying to do so immediately after the first date.

Of course, there will be a lot of guys out there that might be shy or hesitant to meet your loved ones because they don't want to make a bad impression and thus ruin their future with you. But in these instances, their discomfort and reluctance is coming from a place of vulnerability and enthusiasm about being with you. Learn to know the difference based on the situation.

If a guy ignores your requests to have him meet your friends and family and consistently avoids any sort of outings with you that might include them, he's not interested in getting to know you past the temporary little romance-bubble you share together. It's safe to say that once the bubble pops, where he gets bored with you or finds someone new, he's as good as gone.

7

He withdraws emotionally (or physically) at the mere talk of commitment or when you ask him, *"Where is this going?"*

Unless a man is really desperate for a girlfriend or he's one-hundred per cent sure about what he wants, don't expect him to be overly ecstatic when you start mentioning talks of commitment and sharing a life together if you've only been on a mere handful of dates. Most guys know better than to continue seeing a woman (or if he does continue to see her, he'll just use her to pass the time) who seems far more interested in getting a boyfriend than she is in actually getting to know the guy she's just begun dating. No man in his right mind who has just met you wants to feel as if he's on your fast moving conveyor belt to boyfriendom.

Now, with all that said there should come a time when you feel comfortable placing your cards on the table in the hopes that he's willing to do the same. After you really get to know a guy (and seriously, why would you want to make someone your boyfriend whom you barely know?) and you're convinced that you may have something special, don't be shy about letting him know how you feel and what it is you want, which is a committed relationship.

If he tries to avoid the topic or he becomes irate at

the mere mention of your desire for a commitment, this is a red flag. It's an even bigger red flag if he seems to disappear off the face of the earth after you try to DTR (define the relationship) with him.

Granted, I understand that this is tricky territory for a woman because you want to be clear and honest with your needs and wants but you don't want to frighten a great guy into thinking you're desperate and "boyfriend crazy." But even so, the risk of wasting your time and succumbing to a man's on-going seduction is too great to play it safe. If you've gotten to know each other pretty well and there seems to be a whole lot of mutual respect and attraction for one another, don't be afraid to have the talk if you're becoming deeply invested in him.

I always advocate that a woman should be clear with men about her expectations of exclusivity, especially if she's beginning to feel deep emotional stirrings for a guy and she desires to see more of him and get more of his attention. Having strong personal boundaries and clear dating expectations are extremely important. Especially so in this day and age where many women, specifically those who tolerate ambiguous male interest, tend to fall prey not only to Players, but to well-meaning yet irresolute men.

If you've gotten to know a guy pretty well, maintained your dignity, and placed your cards on the table, don't hate yourself if the guy in question pulls away from you or loses interest. It was simply a mismatch of interests and a lack of compatibility. The key to winning with men in order to find the right guy is to be authentic with them as much as possible. You do this by sticking to your standards while being worthy of and willing to express your need for a man's unwavering commitment.

If expressing your desire for an exclusive relationship (after a reasonable period of time of course) causes a guy to disappear, don't fret. I know it sounds cliché, and you might not realize it at first, but trust me…you're better off. You want to be with a man who wants what you want – both you AND a commitment. Ensure that the guys you come across are fully aware that those two things come in one package and that *you* can't be bought separately.

8

He's stubborn beyond reason and inflexible to any changes in plans that might ruin his well-structured life.

Naturally, as a relationship evolves beyond mutual fondness and attraction, you'll want to spend more time with your potential beau. You'll want to become more involved in his world, and have him become more involved in yours. And the more electrifying the chemistry is between you two, the more you'll want to escalate his emotional attachment to you.

This is the natural evolution of a burgeoning romance.

However, if the guy you've become completely

enamored with seems rigid and inflexible to this natural evolution…this could be a major red flag. If he's beyond stubborn and doesn't share your enthusiasm to do something as simple as spend more time together (especially after a month or two of casual dating), this could be an indication that his interest in you is much lower than what you thought it was. It also indicates that you're not a priority for him at the moment, and that he'd rather enjoy you casually than committedly.

Sometimes, men who are extremely ambitious and laser-focused on their careers/businesses might display this sort of behavior. Of course, this is no excuse for leading you on, especially since a guy like this might change his priorities *very* quickly when the right woman comes along.

Also consider that a man who is unwilling to be flexible with you to accommodate your needs (assuming they're reasonable) is too self-absorbed at the moment to provide you with the kind of fulfilling relationship you're looking for. He might be fun, charming, ambitious, and know how to make you smile like the Cheshire Cat from Alice in Wonderland, but that doesn't mean he's ever going to be "all in" with you. A self-absorbed man will pay very little attention to your needs and he's probably hoping to find a woman that will make little to no demands of his time or attention.

I'm pretty sure this isn't the kind of situation you want to find yourself in with a man. Of course, if you *do* consider yourself some sort of martyr, and you don't really care about getting your needs met by a man in any way, a guy like this might be right up your alley.

9

He clearly tells you that he's *"interested in seeing other people"* or that he'd like to keep his options open.

When a man tells you that he wants to keep his options open…believe him and be gone. When he communicates that he's okay with it if you still want to date other people while seeing him…take him at his word then take your business elsewhere. Don't wait around for him to come around and see you as "the one" out of desperation or blind devotion. Maintain your dignity and self-respect by having nothing to do with him.

Men are competitive by nature; thus, securing the **exclusive interests** of a woman becomes a man's top priority once he believes she is a prize-worth-pursuing. If a guy considers you nothing more than an option, no matter how high up his totem pole of options you are, to him at least, you're obviously not a prize-worth-pursuing and committing to.

A man tends to subconsciously appraise a woman's relationship-value based on how she perceives her own value in relation to his own. Put another way, the more desperate you are to be with a man (in this case, allowing him to treat you like an option), the less likely it is he'll ever see you as girlfriend material when he finally decides to commit to a woman. It's a lose-lose situation either way, so why risk the impending mortification and wasted time?

Now, I know for a fact that some women reading this (not you) are going to ignore my warning and give Mr. McDreamy a little more leniency so long as they find him handsome enough, charming enough, wealthy enough, or high-status enough. This is the reason certain men can easily get away with this sort of behavior. Their ability to seduce women, due to their high mating value (attractiveness, confidence, sociability, ambition, etc.) or high-status, makes it easier for them to date opportunistically.

So long as desperate and unwary women abound, guys like this can easily "play the field" at the expense of such women. Don't be a desperate or an unwary woman. And don't believe for a second that a highly desirable yet half-interested man might end up choosing you as the "special girl" that he'll eventually commit to. Challenge yourself not to empathize or make allowances for highly attractive men that use this type of "honest" seduction. There's nothing for you to gain in the long-run by entertaining them, because even though they may appear forthright with you, you're still being used.

10

He prefers to conceal you from the world and refuses to take you out on real dates.

If a man must conceal you from the world for whatever reason, you're in red flag dating territory. This red flag goes beyond him not introducing you to his friends and family. In this sort of situation, he doesn't even want to be seen out with you and prefers to "spend time" with you at your place, his place, or someplace dark and/or distant – usually far away from his regular stomping grounds.

If you're not going out on dates…especially earlier on in a budding romance, you're probably not "dating" in any conventional sense of the word.

There could be numerous reasons why a man might manipulate a situation to keep a romance under wraps. He might already have a girlfriend and would prefer not to evoke her ire and hatred by having her accidently bump into you and him someplace. On the other hand, he may simply not care enough about a future with you to step his game up and woo you like a prize-worth-pursuing.

When a man is dating a woman he considers a prize-worth-pursuing (and he doesn't already have a girlfriend or a harem of women he's trying to "manage"), he'll be eager to show her off to the world. Men are very logical in their thinking and we tend to make decisions based on our top priorities at the time. Therefore, if a man is aware that he's just passing time with you, it won't make any sense for him to make any serious effort to date you. A lack of enthusiasm to go out or be seen with you in public, on his part, should be a clear indication that he's not that interested in you.

Now, don't be misled by this sort of situation. A guy who doesn't want to go out with you might still be very affectionate, caring, and charming. He might even text and call you consistently, as well as make thoughtful gestures to brighten up your day and give you butterflies. This is nothing more than misdirection.

By doing these things, a man can keep you interested enough to stick around but confused enough so that you don't realize the relationship (if you want to call it that) is not progressing. It may "feel" like it has momentum because of the attention he lavishes on you, but don't confuse being treated as a mistress with being treated as a girlfriend. There's nothing wrong with things starting off low-key and casual, but if he's *really* interested in you, the relationship should show some progression towards becoming a blossoming courtship.

So while his displays of tenderness may keep you interested and ultimately confused about his interest, don't be deceived. If the burgeoning romance is sweet in its secrecy, it should be even sweeter once it's out in the open. When a man has commitment on his mind, the last thing he wants to do is isolate you from the rest of his world. If he cannot enjoy your company out in the open, you shouldn't allow him to enjoy it privately either. Read that last paragraph again.

11

He goes to great lengths to avoid any kind of PDA.

Unless he has some sort of weird hang up about being affectionate in public, consider it a red flag if your new guy goes through great lengths to avoid PDA (public display of affection) with you. Why is this a red flag? It's a red flag because a man who is *really* interested in you *wants* to be seen with you in a way that makes it clear that you *belong* to him.

Public displays of affection don't have to be loud and in your face. Some men aren't comfortable with things like passionate kissing when out in public. A few guys might even be averse to having you sit on their laps for long, extended periods of time. However, things like holding hands, a soft kiss on the cheek, and tender touches are generally far more acceptable to most men. Therefore, a man shouldn't have a problem illustrating his affections for you in any of these subtle ways if he believes you're a prize-worth-pursuing and he truly feels honored to be with you.

If he doesn't think you're a prize and he's somewhat ashamed of you, he'll avoid PDA outright so that no one can even remotely mistake you for his girlfriend. On the other hand, he might not have a problem displaying public affection so long as there's no chance of him meeting *other* women. His lack of PDA at a social gathering packed with other beautiful women could be an indication that he doesn't want his potential clientele to think that he's already taken. If he seems hell-bent on treating you like his cousin or some platonic friend that won't stop following him around, he's doing so to appear single to other women.

It sounds harsh, but this is the reality.

Don't be so quick to rationalize a man's avoidance of PDA with you. Yes, a lot of guys have an issue with it, but you'd be surprised at how many still compromise to make you feel secure, loved, and *wanted*. As with everything else, if you're not sure what the reasoning is behind a man's lack of PDA, ask him about it.

Be open, be vulnerable, and listen to what he has to say. If he doesn't show PDA but he goes to great lengths to make you feel loved and adored through his consistent, committed actions, it's all good. If he doesn't show any kind of PDA and he displays many of the other behaviors mentioned in this book, he's not that interested in you.

Chapter Two:

<u>You're Dating A Man-Boy</u>

12

He rarely calls to make plans but prefers to text you. All. The. Time.

Ladies, this is an incredibly easy red flag to spot if you're willing to ignore a man's emotionally stimulating, flirtatious texts and *really* pay attention. If a man's method of communicating with you doesn't seem to be evolving with time, meaning he doesn't graduate from texting to actual phone calls, there's a chance that he's trying to keep things loose, casual, and undefined as long as he possibly can.

For a guy who's just trying to feel you out to gauge your level of desire for him, text messaging is a marvelous tool. By texting you, Mr. Player can communicate effortlessly with several women at once and gauge their responses to determine which of his "girls" is the most high-reward, low-effort pursuit. Granted, all guys who text instead of call you won't fall into this category, but the premise remains the same: When a man is serious about you he'll be more apt to communicate with you like a mature adult who wants to cultivate an adult relationship.

Texting your guy back and forth in the early stages of dating is all fine and dandy, but as he gets to know you a bit better he should be enthusiastic to get on the phone with you. High-quality men know that calling a woman on the phone will at least separate them from the "man-boys" out there that seem to have forgotten the way of men.

Once you've been on several dates and have been seeing him for several weeks, it's okay to up your standards and actually *expect* him to get on the phone with you more often and communicate like an adult. If you've **gracefully** expressed to your potential beau that you would prefer it if he began calling you instead of just texting and he chooses to ignore you...take your business elsewhere. A man that won't make the effort to call you, especially after you've expressed a desire for him to do so, is clearly not interested in cultivating relationship comfort with you, and therefore, not interested in a commitment to you.

13

He doesn't have a job, career, or some sort of legal pursuit that adds value to the economic marketplace.

Ever read the biblical book of Genesis? Ever noticed that in the creation story God gave Adam a job before he created Eve? It seems that even since the beginning of time the relationship between man, his work, and his woman had already been established and given a proper sense of order. Whether you're a big fan of the good book or not, from my life experiences and those of countless other men, I can honestly say that it's extremely difficult for a man to take on the responsibilities of being a great boyfriend (and potential future husband) if he isn't already engaged in some sort of work.

As a general rule, men tend to focus on finding "The One" (the girl whom they want to eventually marry) only after they've gained some sort of career or financial success that makes them feel valuable in the socioeconomic sphere. This doesn't mean that he needs a certain amount of money in the bank or a certain position at his job to take a woman seriously, but it does mean that he's less likely to do so if he isn't at least engaged in financially rewarding or meaningful work.

With that in mind, you can only imagine the loose and super casual dating habits a man might have if he isn't working at all. But if you can't imagine it, let me lay it out simply for you: If you're dating a guy who isn't working, there's a high chance you're nothing more than a beautiful distraction to pass the time.

Now, some women tend to fall into the trap of dating men who are down on their luck, i.e. jobless. These are the women that love the idea of being with a "fixer-upper"; the kind of guy that they believe simply requires a "good woman's touch." Unfortunately, if a man isn't doing all that he can to make himself valuable to the marketplace, no amount of a "good woman's touch" is going to be enduringly helpful. If he had to rely on you to transform him into a man of value, he may end up relying on you indefinitely, or at least until he decides that he wants to trade up for a woman he believes is worthy of his new level of success and status.

Of course, being a man's savior may sound appealing to some women because they believe that it's good to be needed by a man. While it's true that you want to play an indispensible role in a man's success, you want to do this by becoming his support, NOT his savior. A woman actually has more enduring value when she plays a supportive role to a man who's **already moving in a positive direction** to achieve his goals and create value in the world.

If he's not moving in a positive direction – meaning he has no goals, little motivation, no opportunities on the horizon, and little to no sign of doing anything about it – he won't be able to entertain an adult relationship with a woman. Any well-meaning woman that empathizes with his plight and falls for his charms and smooth-talk, will only find herself becoming this man's savior.

Being a man's savior means that you've become the crutch, cash machine, and/or coddling mother he runs to anytime life gets hard or when he loses his way. It's a bad idea to go into a relationship with a man who can't or won't help himself. If you have taken on the role of being his savior, you're only handicapping him of reaching his true potential. And to make matters worse, it's a rare chance that the relationship will ever stray away from this particular dynamic. You might find that you've ended up as "the rock" in the relationship and he may selfishly never become yours.

Do yourself a favor and simply avoid getting into a dating situation with a man who doesn't already have a job or some sort of legitimate business to sustain himself in some way. Because at the end of the day, if a man isn't already engaged in work that's either financially rewarding, psychologically rewarding, or both, his capacity to take a woman seriously and commit his all to her is enormously handicapped.

14

He rarely, if ever, follows up on his word.

When a guy tells you that he's going to meet you someplace and doesn't show, and has a flimsy excuse to boot, you have every right to mark it against him especially if you barely know him. If he promises that he would do something with you or call you at such-and-such a time but never does, consider this a red flag. Why? Because it suggests one of two problems:

1. You're not a major priority in his life and he can therefore blow you off or "make it up to you" as he sees fit, or…

2. He has the unfortunate character flaw of being unreliable, as he's nothing more than just another Mr. All Talk-No-Action.

If a man won't follow through with you, it means he takes you for granted. It also means that impressing you means little to him, thus gaining your respect factors in low on his priority scale. A high-quality man understands that if a woman cannot respect him she won't remain attracted to him and therefore cannot fall in love with him. So if a man isn't concerned about securing your respect, he's not concerned about securing your desire for him. And if he's not concerned about your desire, he's obviously indifferent about keeping you around. Read that paragraph again.

Seriously, if a man doesn't do what he said he would do…what good is he really to you anyway? This is one of the most unattractive character traits a man can possibly have, and it is detestable to both women and men. When a man habitually makes promises that never materialize or he tells you that he's going to do something and doesn't, be assured that a guy like this will bring you more stress and heartache in the future than he will happiness.

Prioritize dating men who make following through on their word and being reliable a part of who they are, as these are the kinds of men that are less likely to let you down because of their high integrity and high personal standards. Remember, a man is only as good as his word.

15

You learn that his past dating history is lined with adoration for women that were clearly unattainable.

Some commitment-phobic men are infamous for dating women that were clearly impossible to maintain a serious relationship with. Some of these women might have become swift exes after they realized that they just weren't that attracted to or compatible with the guy in question. While others were simply women that he'd always wanted to date but could never make them take him seriously (or put another way…he was effectively friend-zoned by them).

These women are considered unattainable because they might have been too young, too old, too married (oh the shame), too opposite in terms of lifestyle choice and interests, or even too aware of their own high mating market value and therefore, too out of reach for your guy at the time.

How can this be a possible red flag? Well, it's because nothing screams "I'm unfit to commit" louder than a man who has a history of self-sabotaging dating habits.

If you allow a man to talk liberally about his dating past and you realize that most, if not all of his past flames were either women that were highly incompatible with him or women that never took him seriously, it could be a sign that he's not really looking for a real relationship at all. In fact, this self-defeating behavior could be a sign that something much deeper is driving his dating decisions.

It could be a sign that on a subconscious level, he's not ready to be with a woman he can successfully cultivate a relationship with and would rather have an excuse to keep him out of a serious commitment. What might be most revealing, however, is when you finally place the spotlight on the burgeoning romance you have with him. By doing so you may quickly realize that he has repeated the pattern with you, since, if you're honest with yourself, you're probably "too something" for him as well. Truth is, a guy like this has a lot of maturing to do, but that doesn't mean he's going to avoid passing time with a beautiful distraction in the meantime.

Of course, if he's really honest with you and tells you that he's still trying to figure out what it is he wants out of a relationship…believe him. However, don't take his honesty as an invitation for you to step in and be that "one girl" that helps him to figure things out. Who's to say that after all your hard work of loving him in his confusion he won't leave you after he realizes that you're NOT the woman he really wants?

Don't place yourself in such a precarious position. If you're at a place in your life where you'd like to be with a mature, high-quality man who knows what he wants, then you have every right to ditch someone who's more likely to waste your time.

16

He seems more in love with being 'in love' than actually loving you.

Some guys are actually more in love with the *idea*

of being 'in love' than love itself. These poor, misled fools are usually the product of a relationship education based on Disney films, romantic comedies, pop love songs, and maybe even bad parenting. Guys like this honestly believe that passion and romantic desire is the end all be all of relationships. And if they're not getting enough of it (and there's never enough of it for them), that must mean the woman they're with is not worth pursuing any further.

These guys haven't matured in the way they approach love, romance, and relationships with women. The pursuit of passion and relationship pleasure is the only thing that keeps them interested in a woman. Naturally, as soon as conflict appears or you want a far more serious commitment that requires more of his time and devotion, the novelty of being with you quickly wears off. It's at this point that your fake Mr. McDreamy will begin to pull away from you so that he can continue on his quest for fresh passion in order to feed his addiction for novelty.

Honestly, this is a rare breed of guy, so if you're fortunate you may never have to interact with one of these saps. But if you do come across one, you'll know it. These guys are some of the most unabashed commitment-phobes you'll find. At first he'll charm you, make you swoon, tell you sweet lies, and pursue you with unusual fervor. But as soon as the whole affair gets too *real* for him…he'll be out of there faster than you can say, *"But I thought you said you were in love with me!"*

17

The way he treats you is inferior to the way he treats others.

If a man isn't giving you the kind of treatment that you *know* he's capable of, what you have is a mismatch in what you expect and what you admire about him. A man might treat his friends, family, and even his dog with loyalty, genuineness, warmth, and consideration but fail to lavish these qualities upon the woman he's seemingly interested in.

More often than not, women in this situation stick around longer than they should. Why? Well, it's because they believe that their Knight-In-Shining-Armor has enormous potential and is capable of giving them the kind of love and loyalty they've seen him dispense to others. Unfortunately, this kind of thinking is ultimately…

False.

If a man's admirable qualities do not successfully translate into relationship benefits, you're deluding yourself with false hope. The more you lie to yourself, believing that someday you'll reap the warmth, kindness, loyalty, and attention from your Prince Charming, the more addicted you'll become to his Dr. Jekyll and Mr. Hyde-like behavior. Which then makes it even more impossible for you to see him for who he really is – a master manipulator with a split personality.

Do yourself a favor and refuse to be a man's charity case. And don't be one of those women who endure bad treatment just to keep a willing-bodied man in her life. Remember, you deserve more than the discarded scraps of a man's kindness.

18

Any plans he makes with you are last minute.

This one might be difficult to spot in a new romance since you and Mr. McDreamy must learn to make room in your busy lives to spend time together. But as time progresses however, you'll begin to get a better sense of whether or not the guy you're seeing makes plans to see you ahead of time rather than last minute.

Commitment-phobic men are heavily averse to making plans regarding their time and attention. This is especially the case with their relationships. Commitment-phobic guys are usually the least dependable because there's no guarantee that they'll actually show up. Whatever plans they do make are ultimately at the mercy of their moods. When the time comes for them to follow through on their commitment but they don't feel like it, suddenly everything else is more important to them.

Guys who only make time to see you at the last minute might *seem* merely commitment-averse, but they're actually self-centered and at times, overly anxious. For guys like this, committing to something way ahead of time produces an overwhelming amount of anxiety (fear), which then leads to stress and other varieties of emotional and psychological discomfort.

As human beings, when something makes us uncomfortable we tend to want to avoid it as much as possible, which then leads to good-old fashioned procrastination. Thus, your Mr. McDreamy might be prone to last minute planning because he's secretly terrified of anything that doesn't make it easy for him to change his mind if he's suddenly not "feeling it" anymore.

Unlike a lot of the other points in this book, guys who exhibit this behavior aren't usually out to waste your time or manipulate you. Knowing this might allow you to sympathize (to an extent) with a guy who acts in this way. By first sympathizing with him you can better understand his commitment-phobic behavior. And once you understand the behavior, you'll be more effective at asserting your boundaries with him as you make it clear that if he wants to continue seeing you he needs to make plans ahead of time with you in mind. Do this gracefully of course.

With all that said, it's not your place to entertain immature men who haven't gotten their act together and who seem unwilling to break free from immature and unmanly habits. I say this because this is something I struggled with in the various phases of my dating life. When I <u>decided</u> that I wanted to find and date a woman who was my prize-worth-pursuing, I began to push past my non-committal behaviors. No woman could have done this for me, as it was a conscious decision that needed to be made. Once I <u>decided</u> that I would no longer waste my time dating women I had little long-term interest in, it became massively easier for me to commit more of my time and attention to the ones whom I held in high regard.

Now, I say all this to make one simple point. When a man is in a place in his life where he doesn't want to waste his time or that of a woman's, he'll be less likely to treat you like a last minute obligation. Don't be a man's last minute obligation. It will inevitably destroy your self-esteem and make it difficult for you to recover once you realize he's just using you to pass the time.

19

He disappears for days or weeks at a time without any sort of reason (or if he does have a reason, it's a flimsy, selfish one.)

Major red flag alert! Guys who disappear for days or weeks at a time without a sound reason for doing so aren't that interested in you. No man who wants you to feel secure with him is going to pull a Houdini and disappear in and out of your life unless it's work related. And even in these work related cases he'll still do his best to **communicate with you** and involve you in his life.

It may seem presumptuous to think so, but if a man considers you a prize-worth-pursuing he'll do anything in his power not to mess things up with you. Remember, the more interested he is, the less likely he is to "play-it-cool" or conceal his desire. Of course, this may not always apply to guys who are a bit more experienced with women, since they know that the *more* desire they reveal the less interest a woman might show. But even with more experienced men, they'll have a much more difficult time concealing their eagerness if they have an intense level of interest in you.

If a guy you've been out with a few times (one who's been voraciously texting you and who seemed *really* interested in you) suddenly takes a hiatus from the new romance, he's not concerned about losing you. If he's not concerned about losing you, he either has more interesting options or he simply doesn't consider you his prize-worth-pursuing. If he believes without a shadow of doubt that he can traverse in and out of your life without reproach, he won't respect you. And as I've touted over and over in my books, if a man cannot respect you he will not commit to you.

Naturally, a woman usually finds it attractive when a man does have dating options aside from her. However, the only way you "win" with a man who has options is when he eventually decides to forego those options to secure your love and loyalty. So don't be seduced into receiving a man's scraps, no matter his level of desirability.

Take Mr. Dreamy-Houdini's disappearing acts as a sign that you're not a deciding factor in anything he does. Take it as a clear indication that he thinks your attention comes cheap, and that he believes that *you* believe you're worth his scraps. Remember, men will treat you how you train them to treat you. So don't train one to feed you scraps of his time and attention.

20

He fails to treat you with respect and he does not respond kindly to your deliberate acts of love.

The more determined a man is to 1. Act with integrity with you, 2. Maintain your dignity, and 3. Cherish your offers of love, the more he values being with you. At the risk of annoying you, I'm going to repeat that sentence again because it's *that* important. The more determined a man is to: 1. Act with integrity with you, 2. Maintain your dignity, and 3. Cherish your offers of love, the more he values being with you. Above all the other points listed in this book, this one should be your TOP priority when determining if a man has a fleeting or long-term interest in you.

It may seem like an old-school ideal, but the more willing a man is to show you honor – treating you with kindness, compassion, and looking out for your reputation and well-being – the more he sees you as a prize-worth-pursuing.

In my book, _Send Him A Signal_, I reveal to women that there's one thing that all men need and want from a woman when they're interested in cultivating a **relationship** with her. It's the need for respect and the need to offer respect. A man may need to feel respected by a woman before he can allow himself to fall in love with her, but he also needs to feel respect _for_ a woman before he can commit to her.

In that book, I state that romantic desire is **not** a good measure of a man's interest in you. Paying too much attention to this factor alone will make it difficult for you to successfully assess his true intentions. You must tune in to the way he consistently treats you, and pay extra close attention to how he responds to your deliberate offers of love and loyalty.

A man knows that in order to earn a woman's respect he must _act_ in an admirable way…consistently. He must show himself as both a good man and a man who's good at being a man. If a woman's character (attitudes and behavior) _demands_ respect, her value skyrockets in the eyes of a high-quality man. And as is human nature, we fall in love with that which we value highly.

Try to see your love, feminine tenderness, commitment, and loyalty as high-priced gifts that you're willing to offer to a man who can truly appreciate them. If you "test" a man with small portions of your gifts (thoughtful gestures, vulnerable conversation for deepening intimacy, invitations to spend quality time together, etc.) and he seems either unable or unwilling to reciprocate…take your business elsewhere. His lack of reciprocation clearly communicates that he has little regard for what you have to offer.

The fact of the matter is, even if you're not "in love" with him yet and neither is he "in love" with you, there should at least be a mutual respect for each other. Not being in love with someone is no reason to treat him or her with disrespect and little regard. If a man doesn't treat you in a way that communicates his high respect for and adoration of you, he's not interested in anything serious with you or any other self-possessed woman for that matter.

21

He has unreasonably high standards and expectations for the women he dates.

Some guys have unreasonably high standards when it comes to choosing a girlfriend. And while there's nothing wrong with a man having high standards, be wary of men whose high standards seem either unreasonable or incongruent with who they really are.

In one of the books I've written for men, I discuss the importance of increasing their standards when it comes to finding the right girl to cultivate a relationship with. The idea is that setting a higher standard for the women they date also helps them to become the kind of high-quality men that high-value women find attractive. But in that book I also clearly point out the dangers of going overboard and becoming a dating perfectionist.

A man who leaves little room for a woman to make a mistake with him might actually be nothing more than an undercover commitment-phobe. By setting ridiculously high standards no woman could (or should) ever live up to, he inevitably sabotages every single romance that comes his way. This ultimately leads to his perpetual singleness; something that he probably wants anyway, even if he doesn't realize it. This sort of thinking is a subconscious trap that keeps him unable to commit to any woman he comes across, as he soothes himself with the excuse that he just can't seem to "find the right girl."

When a man tells you that he's looking for "the right girl", this is a good sign that he's at least looking for something serious. However, if he follows this bit of information with an impossible list of qualities and interests a lady should have if she wants to hold his attention, tread carefully. If he demands that his ideal girl have a thorough knowledge of music, singing, drawing, dancing and the modern languages, not to mention a desire to improve her mind by extensive reading (yes…I'm quoting *Pride & Prejudice*), he's probably more interested in dating Leonardo Da Vinci than you.

Be sure to *really* listen to a guy whenever he talks about his ideal mate and what he finds attractive and valuable in a potential girlfriend/wife. Doing so could save you months of wasted time on a man who's clearly not interested in dating mere mortals.

22

He's only there for the fun stuff and the good times.

Some guys are great fun, total charmers, and tender romancers who would do anything to keep you interested in them and make you happy…so long as you're already happy. Some guys are super romantic, passionate memory makers who can leave you with butterflies in your stomach after every encounter with them…so long as you're not inviting them to do something mundane and ordinary. If Mr. McDreamy is only around when "fun" is guaranteed or when you're experiencing good times, you're in super red flag territory.

As a romance progresses, men quickly figure out how valuable you are to them in terms of how much work they're willing to put in to maintain your interest. If he's sold on you, he'll want to spend time with you even when there's no guarantee of fun. A deeply interested man will even tolerate doing things with you that might make him want to chew off his own foot like a trapped Coyote if it meant a chance to escape. Things like going to your ballet recital, attending your macramé convention, or sitting through that Ryan Gosling chick-flick (you know the one) are perfect examples of things a guy might be willing to endure if it meant making you happy.

Let's say you've been dating for almost two months now and things appear to be going swimmingly. You've placed your best foot forward and you feel comfortable with your new love interest enough to invite him to spend more time with you doing everyday things just to have some company. If at this point he consistently turns down your offers to do ordinary things together, this isn't a good sign. If he's not willing to take part in the every day things with you every now and then, how serious is he really?

Relationships aren't so much about seeking thrills, making romantic memories, or even performing grand gestures; they're more about the companionship and intimacy that grows from doing the little everyday things that add up over time. It isn't realistic for a guy to only seek you out for the fun, exciting, and romantic. If he does, he's what you might call a "Relationship Tourist" – he's only with you for the pleasure and amusement.

In the same vein (but perhaps even worse) are the guys who leave you to handle the trials and difficulties of life alone. Let's take the same period of time, two or more months of dating, and add in something unfavorable. It could be something as simple as a downward emotional spiral after losing your job or something more serious like having to stay in the hospital overnight because of food poisoning. During times like these, does Mr. McDreamy stick around and offer his support or does he disappear off the face of the earth only to show up again when the dust has settled? Even if things like this never come up, based on what you've seen from his natural behavior, what do you honestly *feel* he might do?

Give it some serious thought. Because you don't want to end up wasting time on a guy who will bail on you the minute life deals you a bad hand.

23

You've been dating for six months or longer and none of his long-term plans seem to include you.

Men are vocal and very clear in their actions when they have the intention of making a woman an integral part of their future. A very interested AND emotionally invested man will ensure that any plans he makes for the future are done with you clearly in mind. You won't be surprised when he up and jets over to Japan for a three-month business trip because he'll alert you to such a thing way ahead of time, assuming his boss didn't spring it on him of course. Actually, even if his boss does spring it on him he'll take you into consideration before he makes a concrete decision. Assuming you are important to him, a commitment-minded man would always choose to avoid making decisions that could jeopardize the stability of the relationship.

Aside from making plans that don't include you, a

guy who's not serious about you will also exhibit avoidant behavior when it comes to discussing a future together. Either that or he merely entertains the idea of a future with you just so he can lower your guard and get his way with you now, in the present. This happens to women more often than you'd think. It's the reason behind the phrases: *"But I thought he really did like me"* or *"I don't know what happened, he used to say that he could see himself marrying me someday"*, etc.

Honestly though, there are some instances where a man might entertain a future with you without consciously *intending* to lead you astray. In situations like this, the false hope he feeds you is simply a product of his hormones and an immature worldview of love and romance.

You see, even men sometimes get caught up in the heat of a new romance and may overestimate their own level of desire for a woman. Naturally, once the hormones eventually lift (he gets what he wants from you, life gets in the way, you want more of his time, etc.) he might realize that he's not as sold on you as he thought he was. Most guys will NEVER actually work up the courage to tell a woman this, and so many relationships fizzle out where men pull away, suddenly lose interest, and disappear...even after they've fed a woman false hope of some kind of future together.

A man who wants to keep you in his life will attempt to do so by avoiding behaviors or decisions that might make you feel apprehensive about being with him. So when a guy finds himself dating a woman he finds indispensible to his future happiness and success, he's far more likely to plan ahead with her in mind.

If the guy you're dating avoids conversations about the future, seems too good to be true with his hyped-up hope dope about the future, or if he continually makes major life decisions (ones that undoubtedly have the potential to jeopardize the stability of a relationship) without considering how they might affect you, he either doesn't see you as long-term girlfriend material or he's obliviously self-centered and only interested in getting his needs met.

Either way, these are not easy fixes. So you're better off cutting your losses and moving on so that you can find a great guy who wants you bad enough to make you an integral part of his life.

Chapter Three:

Games Men Play To Get Their Way

24

He only spends time with you when there's an opportunity for physical intimacy.

If a guy only comes around when he's guaranteed to get some TLC (tender love and caressing) from you, he's probably not that interested in you beyond this particular aspect of the relationship. If this is the case, it should be clear to you that he sees the relationship as nothing more than his very own personal day spa. He checks in, gets his needs met, and checks out once he's attained his desired level of satisfaction.

When a man sees you as long-term girlfriend material, he will take an active interest in getting to know the real you – mind, soul, and spirit included. If he sees you as a short-term conquest, he'll only be interested in getting to know your body. This sort of male behavior shows itself in how assertive or insistent he is about establishing an **exclusively physical relationship** with you. If he makes you feel like a piece of meat that can easily be replaced, he's probably hoping to turn you into a friend-with-benefits or an on-going hook-up. You've been warned.

25

He finds major fault in the insignificant and criticizes every little thing you do.

When a guy goes from adoring you at first to suddenly fault-finding, nit-picking, and generally making you feel more reviled than Gollum from *The Lord Of The Rings*, he's trying to get you to do his dirty work for him. What kind of dirty work you ask? Simple really. He's trying to create an overwhelming amount of angst and negative tension in the relationship so that you become incensed with him and eventually take your business elsewhere.

Guys like this are usually highly indecisive, and thus, would rather get *you* to make the final decision. It's a win-win for them actually. Why? Well, if *you* decide to stick around, he gets to "enjoy you" and waste your time without the guilt, knowing that you willingly chose to remain in a messed-up situation. But if you decide to leave, he believes he still wins because he didn't have to do the dirty work and he gets to look like the victim. This sort of behavior is definitely a device of cowardice men; those who don't have the guts to actually tell you that they are no longer interested in seeing you anymore.

Of course, every time a man complains about you doesn't necessarily mean that he's trying to create an exit. But how do you know for sure? Easy. If **nothing** you do is ever good enough, you can be sure he's trying to force your hand. You can take this even a bit further by asking yourself, "Is he complaining about things he already knew and once appreciated about me and are they factors that I have zero to little control over?"

If a guy first met you "as you are" then suddenly finds it necessary to point out that the "as you are" is not conducive to his happiness…he's making an excuse not to be with you. For example, if he met you as a fun-loving socialite and after two months of dating he begins to incessantly harp on your passion for being out in the public eye, he's looking for an easy exit. If he met you Asian/Indian/Black/White/Martian, etc., and after several months of adoration and non-stop romance he suddenly starts hinting at how "women like you" aren't really his type and that he "never saw himself settling down" with a woman of your particular race…he's looking for an easy exit.

The same thing applies if he comes out of nowhere with complaints about your religion, social status, body type, age, or your children (assuming he was fully aware of these things from the beginning). For some guys, it's a lot easier to compel their beautiful distraction to lose interest and leave than it is for them to be the one who calls it off. This is especially true if calling things off with you might make them appear shallow or deceitful. Some guys will go to great lengths to avoid being seen as the "bad guy." They'd rather make it seem as if they're the victim in their little game of seduce 'em and leave 'em.

26

More often than not, he threatens to leave you whenever you're in the middle of a relationship conflict.

Whether it's a man or a woman, if one person in a relationship is constantly intimidating the other with threats of leaving, it's a flashing warning sign that something is seriously wrong. I can't imagine a self-possessed woman with a strong sense of identity and personal confidence falling prey to this form of treatment, but unfortunately, this sort of situation is common for a lot of women.

Threatening someone that you're going to leave the relationship is nothing short of manipulation. If a guy constantly does this to you in the midst of your lovers' quarrels, it's clear that he's more interested in getting his way with you than solving any relationship issues. This is especially true if he's trained you to succumb to his will by threatening to blow up the relationship.

What this sort of manipulation should tell you is that he's not really that interested making you happy, which therefore means he's not interested in a mature and loving relationship. It's a major red flag if a man clearly communicates that he can easily walk away from you without so much as a second thought. It shouldn't matter to you if he's bluffing or not. The mere fact that he has the audacity to use such intimidation to keep you hooked on him should cause you to re-evaluate your choice in men.

Don't make someone your world when you're clearly just an option. And don't stick around, walking on eggshells with a man that might be one argument away from breaking your heart. As a woman, this is perhaps one of the fastest ways to deplete your self-esteem and surrender your dignity to a man.

27

He doesn't believe in titles.

Many men, especially the more experienced ones, wreck havoc in the lives of women as they use their manipulative sweet talk to reap the benefits of being the boyfriend without actually being the boyfriend. They do this by expressing their desire to enjoy a relationship without putting any kind of label on it, relying on their straightforwardness and vulnerability as tools of seduction to lure you into their web of no-strings attached romance. (Of course, this isn't an issue if you don't care about titles either, but since you're reading this book, I'm making the assumption that you *do*.)

When I was in the date around/play around phase of life, I had mastered the art of the "No Title Non-Relationship." So believe me when I tell you that unless you're interested in dating a man casually with no binding commitments or allegiance to one another, do not entertain a man who says that he "doesn't believe in titles." This, my dear, is simply a subtle way for a man to say *"I like you, I'm attracted to you, and I want to have fun with you…but just don't rely on me if life gets tough...because, well…you're not really my girlfriend."*

Now, there might be those rare occasions where you find yourself dating a guy who has recently come out of a long-term relationship with a woman that was deeply important to him. In some instances, a guy a like this might be extra hesitant to enter into anything serious with another woman so soon. The emotional wounds from the breakup might still be too sore, or perhaps he's actually numbed his emotions to the point of becoming disinterested in anything but short-term romances. The things is, only you can tell if a guy in this situation is genuinely interested and wants to take his time, or he's simply in need of a rebound to get him back on his feet and pass the time.

However, even if it *is* true that he just came out of a tumultuous breakup, he's not going to use the phrase *"I don't believe in titles"* to communicate his hesitancy to make you his girlfriend. Such a phrase is the primary relationship-rebuffing tool of time wasters, players, and commitment-phobes alike. So unless he sincerely wants to "take things slow" with you because of a recent heartbreak, don't be fooled by men who blatantly say *"I don't believe in titles."*

28

He loses interest in you whenever you 'lean' into him, and gains more interest in you the moment you 'withdraw.'

Some guys like to go real hard at the beginning of a new romance, but then lose steam the minute they believe they've attained your undivided attention and amorous desire. In a situation like this, you'll find yourself being wooed by an ardent and passionate pursuer, one who appears to be sold on you and who has no intention of letting up so that he can get what he wants. Except he *does* let up, the moment he gets what he wants.

With a guy like this, as soon as your attention switches completely (or even partially in some cases) to him and he feels as if you're his for the taking, he loses interest. What you need to realize is that he was never really after "you" or a "relationship" in the first place. What he really wanted was an intense *desire* for your attention. Or put another way, all he really was after was nothing more than the thrill of the hunt. This particular specimen thrives on the novelty and excitement of a new romance and is more interested in the conquest of love than love itself.

This is an easy red flag to spot because his actions will be loud and immensely clear. When a guy is more interested in the game of seduction than actually being with you, his interest in you will appear very unstable and overly dependent on how much attention you're giving him. The less attention you give guys like this, the *more* they want to be with you and only you. The more you give in to their apparent longing for you, the *less* interest they'll begin to show.

Interestingly though, sometimes guys like this can be "seduced" into a relationship if you're willing to put up with the amount of legwork necessary to keep them engaged. This is why "playing" hard-to-get tends to work in some cases, because there are many guys out there that need to be "gamed" into a commitment. I'm of the opinion however, that while a woman should use *some* cleverness to keep a man interested, she shouldn't take on the role of being a puppeteer-pursuer – one who appears to be "the pursued" but she's actually manipulating the entire seduction process.

If a man isn't showing a clear and consistent interest in you, why bother? Granted, sometimes a woman has to withdraw in order to encourage a man to give chase once again, but this shouldn't become something of a habit just to keep a guy engaged. If you quickly come to realize that the only way to keep a guy interested is to ignore him indefinitely, take your business elsewhere.

Not allowing yourself to lavish your love upon a man who deeply wants you is not only insane, but it's also the fastest way to dating frustration. Don't create a prison of unhappiness for yourself by entertaining men who are irresolute in their desire for you.

29

He keeps you close enough to give you hope, but far enough to keep you unsure of where he stands while using ambiguity to maintain your infatuation with him.

This one can be confusing and is often one of the most common situations women find themselves in. The main reason is that a guy like this may be consciously playing mind games with you or he may genuinely not know what he really wants. If he's playing mind games, it's usually easier for a woman to take her business elsewhere. However, if his interest seems genuine but inconsistent…things might get confusing for her.

Let's address the first instance, where he's consciously playing mind games to keep you addicted to being with him…

When a man realizes that you are the woman he wants for the long-term, his interactions with you will do two things: 1. Stoke your romantic desire for him, and 2. Create relationship comfort. On the other hand, when a man only wants you for the short-term, or when he's "on the fence" about you, his interactions with you will be only one of these two things, namely: To stoke your romantic desire for him.

If he doesn't see you as his long-term goal, he won't be motivated to interact with you in a way that establishes your emotional security in him (relationship comfort). Instead, he will prioritize actions that will keep you happily addicted to him, thus blinding you to his true intentions. Things like calling you often, making plans to see you, being consistent with his displays of adoration will not exist if his only interest is your romantic desire.

In fact, the reverse is true. The less he calls you, the more you'll chase him to see him. And the more inconsistent he is with his displays of adoration, the more intensely you'll burn for him. This is especially true if you haven't yet trained yourself to be repulsed by such male behaviors.

Let's now discuss the second instance, where a guy may seem ambiguous in his interests if he doesn't know what he really wants. If this is the case, he might not be such a terrible guy overall. But why should you waste time and settle for a guy who's "not that terrible"? It doesn't matter if he doesn't know what he wants…you know what you want, and you'd prefer to be with someone who also wants what you want – a relationship. And it's not your job to figure it out for him or stick around **indefinitely** until he figures it out on his own.

30

He's hell-bent on changing some aspect about you (appearance, friendships, career choice, etc.), or that he can't truly love you unless you change for him.

Trying to change you is either a sign that your Mr. McDreamy is a control-freak who might be one bad mood away from domestic violence, or that he doesn't accept you the way you are and is therefore, unhappy with you. When a man nit-picks at the things that make *you* who you are, it's a sign that he doesn't respect or value your individuality.

You can tell if this is a situation you're facing based on the level and nature of criticism you might be receiving from the guy you're dating. For some guys, the act of breaking down a woman who genuinely wants to be with them just so they can recreate her to their own liking gives them a sense of superiority and dominance. These are the control-freaks that can possibly make your life a living hell if you don't realize that their "constructive" or "compassionate" criticism is nothing more than a veil to mask their true manipulative intentions.

Guys like this have an ideal woman in their minds, and if they can't find a woman that fits the ideal they'll try to create one that will. The worst part about this is that if you so happen to allow him to transform you into his ideal girl, there's a high chance he'll lose interest in you and move on to a new "experiment."

Now, keep in mind that there's nothing wrong with a little criticism, since this is a normal part of a budding relationship. As human beings we all have wants and needs that will clash with the wants and needs of others. If your new beau is telling you that it bothers him when you "have a little too much to drink" at social gatherings, this doesn't necessarily mean that he's trying to control you. Always take into consideration the criticism you're receiving to see if it is both just and genuine. It's important to understand context when you find yourself on the receiving end of a man's criticism. A man who's deeply interested in you could be looking out for your best interest in some cases, so don't disregard *all* forms of criticism from a man as controlling or manipulative.

With that said, be wary of any guy that *demands* or *insists* that you change something about yourself or your life in order to make him happy or make him stick around. This sort of Faustian bargain will slowly decay your feminine soul as well as your happiness. If a man seems more interested in controlling you or making you conform to his standards, he's more interested in what he can make out of you than he is in you.

31

He uses language that conveys his unavailability.

When a guy uses self-defeating language to convey his "commitment issues", it's an attempt to gain your trust so that by sympathizing with his complicated emotions your interest in him escalates. Gaining your sympathy in this way also excuses him from any guilt he might experience while leading you on. If he *did* tell you he wasn't "relationship material" and you *still* decided to continue seeing him…was it really his fault that you wasted your time on him?

If the guy you're dating consistently uses discouraging and apathetic phrases when it comes to committing to a serious relationship with you, take this as a clear sign of a lack of serious interest. Here are a few examples of phrases guys might say to covertly manipulate your interest:

- I'm not relationship material.

- You're too good for me.

- I really like you, but I don't want to lead you on.

- I'm not ready for a relationship…but I can't stop thinking about you.

- I don't want to ruin what we have.

- I'm a bit too intense in relationships. I don't want to scare you off.

I'm sure you can add quite a few to this list as well if you've been in a good amount of dating situations with men who were only interested in passing time with you. Hopefully, from this point on you'll know exactly where you stand with a guy the minute you hear one of the above statements or anything even remotely similar.

Now, the most important thing to remember is that when he communicates his non-availability to you through one of the aforementioned phrases (or one just as similar), do not rationalize with him.

I don't think I was clear enough…

When you hear things like this, if you value your peace of mind, do not rationalize with him. For a man who finds himself interested in you just enough to keep seeing you (on his terms), but not enough to commit to you, having a woman *accept* his emotional complications is basically a free pass to lead her on. When things turn sour and he decides he's done with you, no amount of tears, rage, or cajoling will incite his sympathy because as far as he's concerned, he told you so. In his mind, the fact that you continued dating him in spite of his commitment-phobic confessions is totally your fault…not his. And sadly, he's partially right.

Now, if he says one of these seemingly self-sabotaging statements and you *still* want to give him a fighting chance, ask him, right then and there, to *clarify* exactly what he's trying to say to you. If it turns out that he's just being vulnerable with you to express a real insecurity, let him talk, listen closely, then still continue to tread carefully. This is one of those cases where if his actions *don't* match his words, it could be a good thing. If he tells you he thinks you're "too good for him" but he continues to call you, earnestly date you, and show a real progression in his interest and commitment to you, consider yourself his exception.

By the way, I know it seems romantic and all, but don't count on the idea of being a man's "exception." Your approach to finding the right man should be optimistic, but also *very* pragmatic. The fastest way to end up as a man's pastime instead of his girlfriend is to base all of your dating decisions on the hope of being a man's "exception." Don't fall into the trap of working your tail off to convince an unresponsive, half-interested man that you're his exception.

Chapter Four:

<u>It Was Over Before It Began</u>

32

When you go out to social functions together he ignores you for the majority of the evening.

Consider yourself nothing more than a man's "back up entertainment" if the guy you're seeing has a bad habit of ignoring you at events and social gatherings. The only thing worse than this is if he treats you like a social leper whenever *other* women are around.

I can't imagine a confident, self-possessed woman orbiting a man who barely remembers she's even there with him. But it does happen, and usually because a woman might easily rationalize a man's inconsiderate behavior if she finds him "dreamy" enough. Seriously, don't rationalize a man's behavior, especially if he hasn't already proven himself as reliable relationship material.

Now, there are numerous reasons why a man may either consciously or subconsciously ignore you at a social gathering, but they are all based on this common premise: Spending time with you and being seen with you are simply not his highest priorities.

Obviously, this is bad. But here's why…

A guy does this because he either wants to create the space necessary for him to engage with other women or because he isn't *thrilled* to "own" you. Either way, it's clear that cultivating your confidence *in* him is of little importance *to* him. Remember, when a man wants a relationship his actions will create comfort and security in you and not just sexual attraction alone.

The thing is, when a man has a serious romantic interest in the woman he's seeing he'll want to make it clear to others that she "belongs" to somebody, namely him. You can tell where you stand with a man based on how enthusiastic he is to be seen with you as well as how eager he is to spend time with you at social gatherings. As long as he sees you as a prize worth possessing, entertaining other women becomes a pointless pursuit.

Of course, even if a man has a sincere interest in being with you this doesn't mean that he's going to spend every second with you at a social event. A high-quality man will be sure to keep you engaged and entertained without suffocating you in the process. Men like this understand that you can have too much of a good thing way too early in the dating game.

A high status man with a lot of social capital (or even a guy who knows how to *emulate* high status behavior just to impress you) will make his rounds at a social gathering but will always return to you and ensure that you receive the highest quality of his attention. Giving you some space to "miss him" helps to build the image that he's a confident man with high social value and a strong sense of independence.

So remember, a guy who's serious about you will make it quite clear to others that *you* are with *him*. He won't make you feel abandoned, undervalued, or worse, invisible around other people.

33

He gets angry or indignant when you leave things at his place.

When a man becomes indignant about you accidently leaving your purse, shoes, lipstick, etc. at his place, consider it a sign that he's placed you in the "She Won't Be Around For Long" category. Assuming you're not being a slob or leaving behind something unreasonable (like your lapdog), his display of unreasonableness, while it may illustrate his assertiveness and personal boundaries, also communicates his intolerance to the idea of having any remnant of you in his living space.

Now, being the kind of guy that's very particular about his living space, I can empathize with men that have a hard time adjusting to a woman arbitrarily leaving her personals behind. Some guys, particularly the neat freaks and those of us with highly independent temperaments, take a longer time to settle into relationships. This is especially the case if the woman in question is an "easy nester." You know, the ones that quickly adapt their lives to suit the men they date as they effortlessly settle into a romantic relationship.

Still, although some guys may take a bit longer to

get comfortable with the idea of you leaving stuff over, a guy who has a long-term interest in you will be a bit more reasonable to your nesting behavior depending mainly on the length of time you've been seeing each other and the context of your dating situation. For example, if you've been dating for a while and you live a great distance away, leaving a few toiletries shouldn't be a problem so long as it's done with class.

Be considerate of his particular hang-ups when it comes to him having miscellaneous female paraphernalia in his living space. And be sure to talk things out to get a clear understanding of what his boundaries are and what he's willing to compromise with.

Naturally, because of the variations in men's personalities I admit that this particular behavior might be a bit more difficult to point out at first. But even so, it is safe to say that if you've been seeing a guy for several months and he throws a fit whenever you accidently (or intentionally) leave something by his place for the purpose of **making life easier for yourself**...there's a chance that he doesn't see you as even remotely "permanent" in his life.

34

He consistently disrespects you in front of others and it makes you feel belittled or unappreciated.

Mutual respect should be the cornerstone for any relationship, whether it's a romantic or platonic one. Therefore, it's safe to say that a man who blatantly or even subtly disrespects you in front of others has little concern for your self-esteem and well-being. Of course, there might be the rare occasion where a man may unknowingly do or say something to disrespect you in the company of others. But consider it a colossal red flag when this sort of behavior happens consistently, without provocation, and without any sign that it might change in the future.

I can clearly remember an example of this when I first met the then boyfriend of one of my wife's friends. At first glance, the gentleman in question appeared to be just that – a gentleman. He was from out of town and lived together with my wife's friend, and he seemed to be very caring of her, helpful, kind, and committed to the relationship. However, as they continued to interact in front of me, there was only one thing that seemed to make me slightly uncomfortable: He had no problem voicing his displeasures about her and/or their relationship, albeit humorously, in front of her friends –

people he had JUST met.

Now, I understand that some people are a bit more open and tend to get friendly and comfortable in the front of others rather quickly. And I also understand that it's natural for guys to sometime joke around on the weird or annoying behaviors of their significant others. This is normal male behavior, but it's usually normal male behavior when the group consists solely of men…men who are familiar with one another. The red flag here was twofold: 1. There were other women present (her friends/family), and… 2. We had JUST met this guy.

One would assume that any guy who was looking to really "get in good with the friends and family" would be on his best behavior. A guy who's deeply interested in you and serious about sticking around for the long-term will reserve the "girls-are-crazy, let's-laugh-at-them" jokes and discussions for a time when they've already wowed and wooed your friends and family. The fact that this guy didn't do this communicated that:

1. He didn't care what anyone thought of him, or…

2. He simply lacked the kind of thoughtful devotion that would have compelled him to be on his best behavior in front of those who didn't know him yet but who already knew and cared about his girlfriend.

The humor-masked jabs he made at his girlfriend and the relationship had an undertone of disrespect that left me both curious (being the relationship writer-researcher that I am) and a bit conflicted. It wasn't enough for me label him negatively, but it did register in the back of my mind as "atypical" behavior for a man in his situation, as he should have been on his best behavior to earn our stamp of approval.

The unfortunate ending to this was that the guy in question wasn't as enamored with nor committed enough to my wife's friend to stick around when things really got tough. Shortly after, we heard stories of his fierce temper, displays of contempt, and short patience with her, which eventually culminated in him leaving her.

Most unfortunate.

Now, hindsight is always twenty-twenty and it would be unfair to judge a situation based solely on the way a man treats a woman in front of her friends and family. However, you'd be remiss not to take this as a cautionary tale. I've been introduced to all sorts of "boyfriends" of friends over the years, and I've been in the position of being introduced to the friends and family of many girlfriends. I can guarantee you that it is **highly uncharacteristic** for a man to disrespect you in front of your friends and family, especially if he wants to show them his commitment to you in order to attain their stamp of approval. You've been warned.

35

He's a narcissist.

The narcissist is simply unfit for a romantic relationship with another human adult. That is of course, not until they get their act together and go on a serious journey of personal transformation first. You do not want to end up in a romantic relationship with a man that has serious narcissistic tendencies.

But how do you know if your potential Mr. McDreamy is a narcissist? Well, based on the research of the American Psychiatric Association's, *Diagnostic and Statistical Manual of Mental Disorders, Fourth Edition, Text Revision*, [1] individuals with Narcissistic Personality Disorder are defined as having a combination of at least five of the following nine characteristics:

1. Has a grandiose sense of self-importance (e.g., exaggerates achievements and talents, expects to be recognized as superior without commensurate achievements).

2. Is preoccupied with fantasies of unlimited success, power, brilliance, beauty, or ideal love.

3. Believes that he or she is "special" and unique and can only be understood by, or should associate with, other special or high-status people (or institutions).

4. Requires excessive admiration.

5. Has a sense of entitlement, i.e., unreasonable expectations of especially favorable treatment or automatic compliance with his or her expectations.

6. Is interpersonally exploitative, i.e., takes advantage of others to achieve his or her own ends.

7. Lacks empathy: is unwilling to recognize or identify with the feelings and needs of others.

8. Is often envious of others or believes that others are envious of him or her.

9. Shows arrogant, haughty behaviors or attitudes.

Naturally, depending on whom you ask or what books you research, these characteristics take on various different forms in an intimate relationship. For example, in terms of lacking empathy, the narcissistic man will exhibit a lack of thoughtfulness and may be completely inconsiderate of how his behavior affects others. Without empathy we cannot sympathize with others, and we therefore won't be able to act from a place of deep concern and compassion. This makes him insensitive to your needs, wants, and desires, and unwilling to compromise in any way, shape, or form. Also, because of his lack of empathy, don't expect the narcissistic man to show any sign of remorse or shame if his actions prove hurtful to others, including you.

Also, as he may require excessive admiration from others, the narcissistic man will go to extreme lengths to ensure that others' impression of him remains as favorable as possible. While we all want others to think highly of us, the narcissist employs manipulative and dishonest strategies in order to maintain the illusion of his perfection. A perfect example of this is a guy who not only berates you for telling a group of mutual friends about him cheating on you, but he also threatens to ruin *your* reputation if you continue to spread the truth about him.

In another example, because the narcissistic man may, though not always, be extremely charismatic and very socially adept, he might be prone to being interpersonally exploitative. Though a high-level of charm is not a bad thing in and of itself, for the narcissistic man, such personal magnetism is predominantly used for selfish ends. Such a man uses his highly attractive and persuasive personality for one simple Machiavellian purpose: To get his needs met at the expense of others.

The biggest problem for a woman dating a narcissistic man isn't the fact that he might not be that into her...he's just *way* more into himself. Any attempt you make to squeeze even an ounce of thoughtfulness, consideration, and empathy out of such a man will almost certainly be met with a determined defiance. You'll have a higher chance of success negotiating perpetual world peace than trying to get a narcissist to think of anyone but himself.

Author's Note: Consider reviewing the _Diagnostic and Statistical Manual of Mental Disorders, Fifth Edition,_ for a more up to date, albeit far more complex, look into Narcissistic Personality Disorder.

Reference: [1] *Diagnostic and Statistical Manual of Mental Disorders: DSM-IV-TR.* (4th ed.). (2000). Washington, DC: American Psychiatric Association.

36

He still pines for his ex.

No guy who's taken a serious interest in you is going to come right out and tell you that he still misses his ex. You will have to look for those subtle signs of the ex-factor that men exhibit when they are only one love song away from running back to the woman they can't seem to forget.

Of course, you don't want to become one of those weird, creepy women that become over-paranoid when they believe their potential beau is still in love with an ex. Don't go into a new romance fearfully expecting that a man might not be over his ex, because your creepiness will show itself and send him running in the opposite direction. Instead, use discretion and follow these subtle (and not so subtle) signs that your guy might be addicted to the ex:

1. Whether good or bad things are said, her name comes up in random conversations…a lot.

2. He loses his cool and composure when he bumps into her someplace.

3. He can't say "no" to her when she asks for personal favors.

4. You catch him Googling her name (sadly, yes…men do this too).

5. He still has a ton of pictures and other memorabilia of her on his phone, on his computer, or in his home.

6. He gets upset or sad when he finds out she's dating someone else.

7. His mood changes drastically, becoming deeply mellow or even depressed after seeing her

someplace or being reminded of her.

8. His friends tease him about his ex and he starts fantasizing or reliving "the good old days" (you can tell by looking at his giddy, child-like facial expressions).

9. He still keeps in touch with her…a lot.

10. She still comes by to visit him…or his parents.

Honestly, this list can go on and on, but I think you get the picture. You want to be with a man who's emotionally open and ready to move on to something new and real. You don't want to be stuck dating someone who's still haunted by the ghosts of girlfriends past.

Before I entered the serious dating phase of my life, the stage at which I began dating to select a woman I wanted to spend my life with, I had completely gotten rid of anything that was "left behind" from past girlfriends. For some time I had wanted to get serious about the women I dated, but my future expectations were still based on past experiences. I still couldn't seem to shake the emotional residue of girlfriends gone, and therefore I wasn't completely "open" to creating something fresh and *real* with a woman.

Granted, I didn't "pine" for my past girlfriends (and non-girlfriends) in the classical sense. I didn't fantasize or keep in touch with them, but I had so much miscellaneous paraphernalia of them lying around in my living space that I hadn't let go of "what could have been" psychologically. On some level, I understood that to really get the kind of woman and relationship I wanted, I had to get rid of the memorabilia, once and for all.

I found the whole process psychologically cleansing and emotionally freeing. And with my mental and heart space free of the ghosts of girlfriends past, I was able to approach my future relationships with much more openness and maturity. (By the way, I'm never ever going to use the term "heart space" ever again...so enjoy that last sentence while you can.)

When an exes' name consistently comes up or she still remains an active part of his life or even his psyche...tread carefully or just to be safe, don't tread at all. Many women have ended up in situations where they've dated a man (and even married in many cases) that could never give their all and love them completely because of an emotional stronghold an ex had over them. If you really like the guy and you think an ex might be a problem, confront him about it, but do so in a graceful and understanding way. Let him talk and allow him to be real with you, without judgment.

After hearing him out, if you get the impression that there's hope for your guy yet and you'd like to keep him around, do so, but don't settle into a false sense of security. Continue to keep an eye out for those telling behaviors I listed earlier. If over time you still feel insecure about his feelings for his ex and your female intuition screams violently at you telling you that he'll never be completely yours...listen to it.

37

He cheats on you or prioritizes other women above you.

Obviously, only a man who's your boyfriend can cheat on you right? Not necessarily. If you've just began seeing a guy and you catch him making out with some other woman, you *may* choose to overlook this (assuming he's honest and apologetic about it) because there was never any discussion of exclusivity or serious commitment.

But let me challenge that decision.

Did he at least have the courtesy to tell you that he was dating other women? Did he at least consider *your* feelings enough to be upfront about the other ladies that he was romantically involved with? No, he didn't. Which means he's not that concerned about maintaining your dignity and therefore he's not that interested in you.

Of course, we can argue about whether he was in the wrong or not until the cows come home, but this isn't about "right" or "wrong." You've been dating several weeks and you've caught him making out with another woman. He didn't do anything "wrong" because technically, he's not your boyfriend. But in this context you shouldn't be concerned about the technicalities; you should be more concerned about his integrity. Based on an early occurrence like this…can you really trust this guy moving forward? Think about it.

On the other hand, if he's already your boyfriend and you find out that he's cheated on you…be done with him, for good. You're not married, and you therefore have no strong enough reason to try and pick up the broken pieces and make it work. At present, it's broken beyond repair, smashed to dust, and you need to disengage completely and move on. I'm being cruel to be compassionate here, and I say this with the utmost earnestness.

If your boyfriend cheats on you – and by cheating I'm talking about *any* kind of physical intimacy with another woman – be done with him. Remember, you're reading this book to learn how to filter for a man who will want and cherish you for a very long time (even a lifetime). Sure, he may change his ways and never do it again for as long as he lives, but is that a risk you really want to take when there are more loyal options out there? Think about it.

38

He always seems self-focused when with you, or worse, he seems as if he'd rather be doing something else.

Consider it a red flag that a man isn't that interested in anything serious with you if he appears to always be self-focused or even "disengaged" whenever he is with you. When a man is seriously interested in you, he will have a sincere interest in *you* and the goings on in your life. Even if he isn't the most attentive guy on the planet, because he considers you a prize-worth-pursuing he will put in the extra effort necessary to remember the small details about your life to prove his genuine interest to you.

To really decipher if a guy isn't "all there" with you, look for signs of personal disinterest. Behaviors that make you feel as if you're nothing more than "background noise" to a man is a clear indication that his focus is either fully on himself or elsewhere. But what are those subtle (and not so subtle) signs of personal disinterest? Because I'm such an amazing guy, I've listed several of them below for your personal benefit. Use the following points as a basis for discovering whether or not a guy is disengaged and therefore, disinterested:

1. He has little to zero eye contact when conversing with you.

2. He shows a lack of interested and/or enthusiasm whenever you're conversing with him.

3. He appears more interested in talking about himself and impressing you than creating a real connection with you.

4. He looks off into space with a face that reads: *"I wish I was anywhere but here right now!"*

5. When he does finally focus on you, he'd rather

let you reveal and share the details of your life with him than reveal anything of his own. This is akin to what I already discussed in point number two, where he's hell-bent on hiding information from you.

6. He communicates with you disrespectfully. Example: He habitually cuts you off mid-sentence to speak his mind, or, fails to make a conscientious attempt to actively listen to you.

7. He doesn't pay attention to the simplest and most charming details of your romance. Example: He can't remember when he first saw you, or, he can't remember the first date, etc.

8. He doesn't pay attention to the goings on in your life. Example: He's met your best friend several times and doesn't at least remember her name, or, he doesn't follow up with you on important things like a doctor visit, college exam, job interview, etc.

If your Mr. McDreamy doesn't want to know more about you, he's just passing time and looking for something to keep him amused. If he really likes you he'll want to get to know you as much as he possibly can. He'll listen intently to you and will go the extra mile to remember the little details.

You'll know just how interested he really is because as the romance progresses you *will* be impressed by how much he actually retains and remembers later on. He'll even use this knowledge about you to go out of his way to either surprise you with a thoughtful gesture, a meaningful dating experience, or even just to make your life a little bit easier in some way.

Remember that men are **generally** less thoughtful and considerate than the fairer sex, at least when it comes to building relationships. The only reason we'll place a woman's well-being at the forefront of our thoughts is when she really means something to us and **we want her to know it**. A guy who takes an interest in knowing *you* and who remembers the details of your life (and uses this knowledge to increase your happiness and well-being) has made you one of his top priorities. If he's not doing any of this, he's obviously not that interested in you.

39

He isn't open to your input, influence, or support.

Men want to be gracefully influenced by the woman they love and desire. At least, this notion applies to high-quality men, those who value the support of a loving and loyal woman. If a man consistently rejects your support or isn't open to your influence and he isn't showing any signs that he might change in the future, he probably doesn't *see* a future with you.

Let's say you've been dating a guy for over a month and an opportunity arises for you to display your womanly support and wisdom. For example, he has several family members (all of them women) coming to town and you go out of your way to offer your help anyway you can. Let's say he rejects your idea of accompanying him to show them around the city for some sightseeing. At first you think that he just doesn't want to inconvenience you, so you offer other ways you can be of help, which, much to your surprise, get shot down as well. If he rejects everything from your suggestion of places they might like to visit to your offer to cook something for him and the group, you have every right to feel at least a bit slighted.

If this guy is *really* interested in you and you display an act of thoughtfulness like this, he won't have to think twice about your offers or suggestions. Actions like this scream "GIRLFRIEND MATERIAL", thus, if a man is unwilling or incapable of recognizing your value in this way…he's probably not that interested to begin with.

(Note: Keep in mind that I'm basing this example on the assumption that you are the kind of woman who doesn't mind putting herself out there to show a man that she's the real deal, or, what men like to call "high-quality girlfriend material.")

This is a simple example to be sure, and the reasons why a man may reject your support or input have to be considered within the context of the situation. But even beyond context, you also want to pay attention to his *consistency*. If he consistently rejects your support, input, or influence, consider it a sign of his low-interest in and little regard for you.

Highly ambitious men who desire success in both their careers and social lives understand that the input of an intelligent and supportive woman is invaluable. Life is full of surprises, conflicts, and unforeseen problems. Accepting this notion, no man in his right mind wants to go at it alone if he can be assured that the woman he loves can help him navigate the rocky seas of life. Not being open to your input or influence is either a sign that a man is uninterested in having you as a part of his life or that he's not yet convinced that you are "the one." If it's the former, you can simply take your business elsewhere. If it's the latter however, this can be a bit trickier to navigate.

You see, before a man can open up himself to a woman's influence, he needs to *feel* assured of her understanding, compassion, and most importantly, her loyalty. He wants to know that she truly has his best interest at heart, and that her input is coming from a place of deep empathy and a desire to see him succeed, thrive, and prosper. If a man gets the impression that your input is coming from a place of self-interest, there's nothing in this world you can do to influence him.

As the gatekeepers of commitment, once the novelty of physical attraction and interpersonal chemistry has worn off, we award our unwavering allegiance and fidelity to the woman who proves herself *least* likely to disrespect us, stab us in the back, wound our egos, or manipulate us for her own benefit. And while today's culture may glorify the me-against-the-world "Loner Hero" male archetype, emotionally mature men understand that the reality is actually the complete opposite. Men like this understand that no man can achieve or get along in this life without the help and influence of others, especially in matters that necessitate the sagacious input and loving support of a good woman.

So keep all this in mind as you interact with the men you date. If, as the relationship progresses, you realize that a man does not respect or value your input, there's a high chance he's not that into you. This is especially the case if you've been dating a guy for several months and he continues to respond to your input and offers of support with irritation, insolence, or abhorrence.

40

His good intentions leave you feeling anxious and insecure.

If a man reveals his good, most sincerest intentions towards dating you and yet you still get a nauseating, gut-level feeling that makes you irrationally anxious about your future with him and whether or not you really matter, this could be your intuition guiding you to see that things aren't what they seem. This may happen when everything a guy says is perfect and reassuring to you, but his actions don't meet up with what he's saying. This is the beauty of your female intuition. **If you let it, it will pick up on a man's incongruence, no matter how subtle, and inform you about his capacity to remain true to his word.** So while a man's vulnerability and genuineness can be quite convincing, you'll never feel at peace with him if his actions do not consistently measure up.

Every human being on this planet has fallen prey to the sincerity of others. Why? This is because someone can be completely genuine, yet completely wrong. Genuineness is not a strong determinant of truth or reliability, and this is especially the case when it comes to romantic relationships.

If you want to succeed with men and figure out which ones are worth your time, you must learn how to differentiate between a man's sincerity (his good intentions) and his integrity (true reliability). Don't confuse sincerity with integrity. You cannot rely on a man with good intentions if those intentions rarely amount to anything measurable or tangible. A man may be sincere with you but lack the integrity to follow through on that sincerity. He may be genuine and yet at the same time be unreliable.

If what a man does simply does not match what he says…there's a good chance it's an integrity problem. He can be as earnest as he wants, but no matter how sincere his intentions, without the proper actions to prove his integrity it matters very little.

Many women tend to fall prey to male sincerity. When a woman becomes smitten with a man it's much easier to overlook those minor faults (and sometimes major) for the sake of experiencing a new romance. No one is perfect of course, and there's nothing wrong with overlooking someone's faults because it helps otherwise imperfect people to come together and cultivate intimate relationships.

However, the problem arises after the 'love' chemicals and hormones have died down and we find ourselves deeply involved in a relationship with a deeply flawed person. A flawed person who failed to meet our expectations, made us promises, and told us sweet lies. Lies that even *they* didn't know were lies at the time.

Sincerity implies an earnestness of good intent. And it is this good intent that fools many women into believing a man…consistently. Assuming a man has honest intentions, whenever you hear a woman say in frustration: *"I can't believe I fell for him again"* or *"I can't believe I thought he'd actually _____ this time"*, what you have is a woman who fell for a man's sincerity.

But why is it so easy to succumb to a man's sincerity? Simple. Sincerity is far more emotional in how it is communicated…integrity is not. Hence why it is beneficial for a woman to learn how to "think like a man" at times, so that she can see a man for what he is rather than what he'd sincerely like to be or even what he sincerely wants her to believe.

For example, let's say that you're dating a very busy, ambitious man who has a lot going on in his career. Let's say he repeatedly calls you *way* later than he promises. As the relationship progresses, you probably understand that because of his hectic schedule, he has a problem following through on contacting you when he said he would. But let's also say that every time he does finally contact you (two or more days later) he has some sad (and convincing) story of why he was late and that he's sorry for doing so and promises to do better in the future.

Except he never does.

You forgive him because you really, *really* like him

and you believe in his earnest desire to be more thoughtful of you in the future, hoping that he'll change.

Except he never does.

So why do you fall for it? It's because he apologizes from his heart, and you know he's probably telling you the truth. Not only that, but he also communicates in an emotional and persuasive way that makes it easy to believe that he has the capacity for improvement, except at this point in his life…he doesn't.

During the dating phase of your life, do not presume that a man has the capacity to do better in the future until he actually *does* better. You can believe *in* him, but don't become a fool for him. The same thing applies if you're in a long-term relationship with a man you truly love and don't want to leave. You can save yourself a ton of frustration by simply learning to separate a man's genuineness from his actual level of dependability.

Now, I used this very light example of Mr. Too-Busy-to-Call just to get the point across. But if you consider larger relationship issues (like being faithful for example) I'm sure you can see how problematic it can be for a woman if she repeatedly falls for a man's sincerity and earnestness as opposed to evaluating his level of integrity.

This is why it is far more important to stay tuned in to what a man does rather than what he *desires* to do. The earlier in the relationship you can access his level of integrity the less stress you'll place on yourself in the future, at least when it comes to your expectations from him.

It's easier to fall for a man's sincerity in the earlier stages of a courtship because the 'love' emotions are high, your hope for the future is overwhelming, and your experience with him is minor. But if you can temper your emotions just enough so that you can quickly assess if what he says matches what he does *more often than not,* you will have developed a masterful **intuitive** skill that can quickly decipher between a man's *words* and his true *worth*. Read that last paragraph again.

This is one of the greatest aptitudes a woman can have, especially early on in her dating life, as it gives her a near flawless tool for filtering through the endless supply of well meaning but unreliable men who might ultimately waste her time.

Final Thoughts

Here's the key to becoming a masterful expert at deciphering the romantic intentions of men: Make being treated with love and respect a higher priority for you than receiving male attention. I say this because the biggest hindrance to weeding out the men who want you for a lifetime from those who only want you for a moment is your own level of fear, anxiety, and desperation. The more desperate you are for male attention the less composure and reasonability you'll have at your disposal when trying to assess a man's true intentions. If you want to filter out the good ones from the guys who only want to have their way with you, you must learn to prioritize quality male treatment over indiscriminate male attention.

It's natural for a woman to want to affirm her desirability through male attention. In fact, the full expression of female sexuality is to attain the complete adoration and the unrestrained craving of a highly desirable man. Keeping this firmly in mind, fighting against your nature isn't the answer to overcoming the manipulative wiles of a desirable man. Instead, it would be in a woman's best interest to become more selective in her taste in men.

If you fail to be highly discriminate with male attention, you'll remain at the mercy of your natural desires.

This might be especially difficult for women who grew up in homes where their fathers were absent (physically and/or emotionally). I know you have probably heard the term "Daddy Issues" before. It's a term used to describe women who have messed up or non-existent relationships with their fathers; the negative effects of which usually stumble into their adult relationships with men.

If your father provided you with little or no attention, there's a high chance that you'll subconsciously seek it out from the men you date in order to fill that void. You'll find yourself putting up with unloving men and dead-end relationships just for the sake of having a guy in your life; one whom you might unfortunately over-value because he was kind enough to take a romantic interest in you (even if that interest is low-quality and inconsistent). Sometimes women like this become addicted to chasing a man because they'd rather be treated poorly and have a man's attention than feel undesirable and alone.

Believe me, you're worth a lot more than the drip-fed morsels of a man's attention. At least, you *should* be worth a lot more assuming you actually believe it yourself. Your interactions with men must communicate your high-value, personal dignity, and self-possession (attributes high-quality men love in a woman) if you want them to take you seriously. The way to accomplish this is to date as if you deserve love, rebuff any male behavior that threatens your dignity, and cultivate a strong desire to be with a man who consistently shows that he wants to be with you and claim you as HIS woman.

Failing to interact with men in this way will make you a prime target for time wasters, game players, and men who just want you for the moment. Why? It's because your interactions with a man will always give you away. A man will ignore your pleas, your petitions for more attention, and your tears so long as your actions are incongruent with what you're demanding of him.

You must want to be treated right by the right man far more than you want male attention. And as cliché as it sounds, this can only be achieved by increasing the love and esteem you have for yourself, and by knowing when to gird your loins and pull the plug on a dead investment or a dead-on arrival romance.

One More VERY Important Thing

As you enter a new romance armed with the knowledge in this book and books like this one, depending on your past experiences with men, you may be tempted to over-compensate. If you've realized that you've been too lenient with men in the past and you allowed them to walk all over you, get their way, and lead you into dead-end relationships, don't fret. You may find that in your zeal to "correct" the way you interact with men, you may make another gigantic mistake: Becoming overly demanding in a new romance or over-stressing a budding relationship.

While you want to ensure that men aren't leading you on, you also don't want to destroy the seeds of a new romance before it has a chance to sprout. Becoming fearful, over demanding, or stressing out will have an adverse effect and cause your potential Prince Charming to run in the opposite direction. So with those women in mind, I've provided this section so that they can keep both their sanity and the interest of their potential Prince Charming.

How to Keep Him Interested Without Losing Your Sanity

Here's the big secret to keeping a man interested in you as a new romance begins to blossom: Know what you want, but **don't stress out** over the relationship.

One of the worse things you can do to a new romance is lose yourself in the fantasy of what the relationship with this guy *could* someday be instead of enjoying it for what it is at the moment. Yes, you don't want him to waste your time or lead you on, but you also don't want to come off like a commitment-consumed cat-lady who's only interested in having a willing-bodied man to cuddle and love.

Men don't want to feel like they're on your conveyor belt to boyfriendom as you process them into a relationship like cattle in a slaughterhouse. We'd much prefer it if you took your time, enjoyed the ride, and happily seduced us into a relationship. Yes, we have feelings too!

"But what about my plans?" you might task. You know, stuff like:

1. Find a good man.

2. Make him boyfriend.

3. Make him propose.

4. Have husband! *Yay!*

Hey, you're entitled to have your own hopes, dreams, goals, and desires for your love life, but everything in moderation. The first two things you must remember about love are that above everything else it is **sincere** and **unselfish**.

Let's address the first…

If you're being **sincere** with a guy, you're acting from a place of genuineness and naturalness. Sure, you can be in it to get a boyfriend and eventual husband, but if your fears, frantic behavior, and anxiety override your ability to act from a place of sincerity, you'll give off the mild, but still very repugnant scent of desperation, neediness, and artificiality. In short, guys will see you for exactly what you are: a woman with an agenda that's *more* important than loving him with sincerity.

Being **selfish** speaks for itself. Just like being insincere, it screams that a woman is all about her agenda. But it does something even worse in that it tells a man that you're only interested in getting what *you* want from a relationship.

Now, I know this all may seem contradictory, especially if a woman is ever going to find a man who takes her serious enough to commit and eventually marry her. Honestly, it IS difficult to balance having strong boundaries and relationship expectations without stressing out over the trajectory of a new romance. So what's a girl to do then?

Fret not, my dear. I have a few suggestions!

Below are three practical ideas that may help you.

1. Treat Each Situation Differently

The first thing is to treat every dating situation differently. Some guys are far more decisive about what they want in life than others. So don't expect every man you date to immediately figure out on your first date with him that he's going to marry you within the month.

The more experience you have with men the more you'll realize that different types of men, at different stages of their lives, will want *very* different things. A guy who's just started his first year of medical school might be less apt to take on a serious relationship than a guy who's just been promoted to regional city manager and has put a deposit down to buy his first home. The stage of life and the level of maturation you meet Mr. McDreamy will play a large role in what he wants out of a romantic relationship.

This is why open communication with a man and being honest with yourself is extremely important. Are you willing to put up with a man who has a demanding career? Can you be extra patient with a man who, because of his age, is relationship-minded but not necessarily relationship-ready yet (an example being a man who has just recently divorced or ended a long-term relationship)?

Give it some thought, and be honest with yourself in the various dating scenarios you find yourself in.

2. Know When to Be Insistent

The next thing is to implement a definite cut-off point. Knowing that you've set an allotted time to "pull the plug" on an inert relationship allows you to completely focus on your new guy as you give him the benefit of the doubt. By having a "you snooze, you lose" dating approach you won't lose your marbles trying to cajole and manipulate a man into committing to you.

But what is a cut-off point? It's basically a point in your relationship where you've decided to make a decision to stay or go based on where a man stands with you, and vice versa. Many other authors and dating coaches have touched on this subject ad nauseam, so I'm pretty sure this isn't a new concept to you. But so many have suggested it because it works AND it helps you to reduce the amount of fear and anxiety you might experience with the guys you date.

If you're going to implement the cut-off point I have two suggestions.

First of all, please ensure that you *know* what this cut-off point is ahead of time. For example, if after two months of casually going-out and getting to know each other and a man hasn't figured out that you're *exclusively* girlfriend material, either move on or give him a chance to correct his ignorance with "the talk." You can be as cutthroat and selfish as you want at that point simply because you've already made a rational and logical decision to "have the talk" with him if you don't see any noticeable progression *after two months*. Remember, if you don't value your time, neither will he.

Now, during those first two months, you would be wise *not* to act in a way that would make you look like you're only interested in achieving a goal. During those first two months **you must not have an agenda**. You must simply *enjoy* his company and be as sincere and unselfish as you're able to.

This leads me to the second caveat: The main thing to remember here is that if you *do* decide to have a cut-off point, you must discipline yourself early on *not* to concern yourself about the trajectory of the relationship *until* you're arriving at your cut-off point. Taking this approach will keep you from sabotaging a potentially great relationship with a great guy. Don't do that. If anything, let him sabotage it himself if he fails to make you his girlfriend.

Not convinced? Think about it this way: If after two months of him getting to experience your warmth and tenderness then you suddenly turn off the faucet to your attention and withdraw from him, if he has even an inkling of serious interest in you he will pull out all the stops to win your attention and ensure that he doesn't lose it again. IF, however, you fail to be warm, relaxed in your femininity, and sincere during those first two months (because of your lack of a cut-off point), you turning off the faucet will merely seem like *more* craziness to him, which, in turn, will make him run in the opposite direction without any regrets.

3. Express Your Desires Early and Candidly

And finally, it's important that you be as candid and honest as possible from the start of any new romance. This is all about dating with a purpose and setting your dating standards high. There is absolutely nothing wrong with a woman expressing her interests in having a boyfriend or that she hopes to be married in the future to a man she loves with all her being. It is my belief that the more open you are about these things early on, the greater your chance of filtering out men who don't want what you want (long-term commitment, exclusivity, marriage, etc.).

This is why having deep, intimate conversations on your dates is so important. You need to get to the heart of a man and figure out *what he's really after* as early as possible so that you don't waste your time (or his). **It makes no sense to have "the talk" with a guy at your two-month cut off point and realize that he had no idea you were looking for something serious.** Being honest with yourself, setting clearly defined dating boundaries, and ensuring that a man is well aware of your desire for an exclusive relationship will increase your chances of ending up with someone who won't lead you on or abandon you.

So if you take nothing else from this book (which I highly doubt), ensure that you at least remember this: Don't be naïve when it comes to men. If you don't express your desires from the start, don't assume that a man is aware of them. When it comes to interacting with women, men are masters at ignoring the obvious in order to capitalize on the unmentioned and exploit the unenforced.

Remember, date as if you deserve love and don't feel bashful about setting boundaries with the men you date. The more principled you are when dealing with men and the more discriminating you are with male attention, the more attractive you become to relationship-minded men. Remember that.

About Bruce Bryans

Bruce Bryans is a successful author who has written numerous best-selling books for men and women who want to improve the quality of their relationships. After writing for various online publications on the topics of dating and relationships, he ran a successful romance advice website where his insightful articles and newsletters helped improve people's love lives one-by-one.

Years later, Bruce decided to focus his time and efforts on writing and publishing books with easy-to-implement, practical information that had the potential to reach, and therefore help more people. While he doesn't consider himself the all-knowing "Yoda" of relationships, he still enjoys sharing the triumphs (and failures) of his love life with anyone who enjoys a good laugh or a life lesson.

When he isn't tucked away in some corner writing a literary masterpiece (or so he thinks), Bruce spends most of his time engaged in manly hobbies or being a romantic nuisance to the love of his life.

You can learn more about his writings and receive updates (and future discounts) on his books by visiting his website at: www.BruceBryans.com

Most Recommended Books by Bruce Bryans:

The 7 Irresistible Qualities Men Want In A Woman: What High-Quality Men Secretly Look For When Choosing "The One"

In <u>The 7 Irresistible Qualities Men Want In A Woman</u>, you'll find out the feminine qualities that commitment ready, high-quality men look for when choosing a long-term mate.

101 Things Your Dad Never Told You About Men: The Good, Bad, And Ugly Things Men Want And Think About Women And Relationships

In <u>101 Things Your Dad Never Told You About Men,</u> you'll learn what high-quality men want from women and what they think about love, sex, and romance. You'll learn how to seduce the man you want or captivate the man you love because you'll know exactly what makes him tick.

Make Him BEG For Your Attention: 75 Communication Secrets For Captivating Men And Getting The Love And Commitment You Deserve

In <u>Make Him BEG For Your Attention</u>, you'll

discover how to talk to a man so that he listens to you, opens up to you, and gives you what you want without a fuss.

101 Reasons Why He Won't Commit To You: The Secret Fears, Doubts, And Insecurities That Prevent Most Men From Getting Married

In 101 Reasons Why He Won't Commit To You, you'll learn about the most common fears, doubts, and insecurities that paralyze men and prevent them from making the leap from boyfriend to husband.

Never Chase Men Again: 38 Dating Secrets To Get The Guy, Keep Him Interested, And Avoid Dead-End Relationships

In Never Chase Men Again, you'll learn how to get the guy you want, train him to pursue you, and avoid dead-end or even "dead-on-arrival" relationships by being more assertive and communicating high-value to the men you date.

Send Him A Signal: 61 Secrets For Indicating Interest And Attracting The Attention Of Higher Quality Men

In Send Him A Signal, you'll learn the subtle signs of female interest that entices men to pursue a woman and also how to become more approachable to high-quality guys.

More Great Books by Bruce Bryans:

If you have a special guy in your life that could use a bit more wisdom when it comes to dating and relating with women, you should sweetly suggest that he check out some of my books. Actually, even if YOU want to learn about what guys are learning about when it comes to understanding women, peruse through my other books listed below.

Attract The Right Girl: The Official Guide For Finding Your Dream Girl And Being The Man She Can't Resist

In <u>Attract The Right Girl</u>, you'll discover how to find and choose an amazing girlfriend (who's perfect for you) and how to spark the kind of attraction that'll lead to a long-term relationship with her.

Find Your Path: A Short Guide To Living With Purpose And Being Your Own Man…No Matter What People Think

In <u>Find Your Path</u>, you'll discover how to find your mission in life and how to become a much more self-assured man of purpose and inner conviction.

How To Be A Better Boyfriend: The Relationship Manual For Becoming Mr. Right And Making A Woman Happy

In <u>How To Be A Better Boyfriend</u>, you'll discover how to cultivate a rock-solid, mind-blowing, romantic relationship with your dream girl, and what to do to avoid all the drama, bad girlfriend behavior, and game playing that many "nice guys" often fall prey to in relationships.

How To Get Your Wife In The Mood: Quick And Easy Tips For Seducing Your Wife And Making Her BEG You For Sex

In <u>How To Get Your Wife In The Mood</u>, you'll discover the relationship secrets used by some of the most blissful couples in the world as well as romantic hacks that'll help you to get all the sex you want from your wife and make it seem like it was all HER idea.

Meet Her To Keep Her: The 10 Biggest Mistakes That Prevent Most Guys From Attracting And KEEPING An Amazing Girlfriend

In <u>Meet Her To Keep Her</u>, you'll learn the ten dating mistakes that stop most guys from attracting and keeping a 'Total 10 girlfriend' and how to overcome them.

What Women Want In A Man: How To Become The Alpha Male Women Respect, Desire, And Want To Submit To

In <u>What Women Want In A Man</u>, you'll learn how to become a high-quality, self-confident man that can naturally attract a good woman, maintain her sexual attraction to you, and keep her happy (and respectful) in a relationship.

Thank You

Before you go, I'd like to say "thank you" for purchasing my book.

I know you could have picked from dozens of books on understanding men, but you took a chance on my guide and for that I'm extremely grateful. So thanks again for downloading this book and reading all the way to the end.

Now, <u>IF</u> you liked this book I'm going to need your help!

Please take a moment to leave a review for this book on Amazon. Your feedback will help me to continue to write the kind of books that helps you get results. And if you so happen to love this book, then please let me know!

36296326R00068

Printed in Great Britain
by Amazon